# Behind the Bar

# Behind the Bar

## Inside the Paralegal Profession

*Catherine Astl, C.L.A.*

iUniverse, Inc.
New York  Lincoln  Shanghai

Behind the Bar
Inside the Paralegal Profession

iUniverse, Inc.

For information address:
iUniverse, Inc.
2021 Pine Lake Road, Suite 100
Lincoln, NE 68512
www.iuniverse.com

ISBN: 0-595-30100-2

Printed in the United States of America

# CONTENTS

# <u>ACKNOWLEDGEMENTS</u>

I would like to thank the following people who supported me, provided me with material, believed in me, inspired me and were there for me, always:

My dear, sweet, husband, Kevin Astl—there will never be enough time to have with you— the love of my life and my dream come true. I adore you more than my simple words can express. Thanks for always, *always* being there for me, and boosting my confidence.

My fantastic, loving parents, Nick and Cathy Abernathy—thanks for the inspiration, support, compassion, talent, self-confidence, logic and sense to make my dreams happen. I truly, "took advantage of all of my opportunities!" but I could not have done it without your backing and upbringing.

Carrie, Tom, Bryan and Steven Fielding—Carrie, my identical twin sister and a truly remarkable paralegal, thanks for listening to me and for some exceptionally "hot" stories! Tom—thanks for your support. Bryan and Steven—you are so precious to me!

Sandra and Alfred Astl—you are always there for me and are wonderful people. Thank you for your support.

My dearest Aunt Judi. Thanks for always being there and for your support. No matter how many miles separate us, we are always together.

My dear Grandmother, Pauline Rogers and my Grandfather, Joey Rogers—I love you both so much.

To the rest of my huge family—Vicki, Gerry, Mike, Mark, Joanne, Paul, "Little" Joey, Lisa, John, Lauren and Sidney—thanks for your support. And to my many wonderful friends, thanks for your interest and encouragement.

# CHAPTER I

# THE LIVELIHOOD OF LEGAL ASSISTING

Behind the Bar is a truly unique vantage point. It is a mountaintop view of the valley of joys, grievances, frustrations, and wonders of our justice system and the human emotions that encase it. Legal Assistants are to attorneys as sherpas are to mountain climbers; the backing, force, and engine behind the scenes of the legal profession to reach its ultimate summit of justice.

As a legal assistant, assisting and supporting members of the Bar—attorneys—as well as others within the field, you have the occasion to be part of a special team where one member cannot function fully, if at all, without the other. Together, a professional and, oftentimes, personal bond forms between legal assistant and attorney to deal with societal problems, dilemmas, issues and disputes.

Though the field of legal assisting, is and has been exploding in growth, many do not truly know what a legal assistant, or paralegal, really is or what they do. Some just believe that paralegals assist lawyers and "do most of the work." For use in this book, I interchange the two terms "legal assistant" and "paralegal," but they mean the same thing. Just as a "lawyer" and an "attorney," or a "doctor" and a "physician;" two different terms, but their modern meanings are the same.

If you are interested in this field, and especially if you are contemplating this career choice, your line of investigation should include finding out as much as possible about exactly what legal assistants do in their day-to-day lives at the office, as well as what an overall view of the profession is really about. With insight and awareness, you can better decide if this type of vocation is the right one for you.

I. When I first started to write this book, I was at the point in my paralegal career and life that we all know as a crossroads, but it was more like a traffic circle, with me going around and around, but never really stopping anywhere or getting back into the flow of travel to move on to the next destination. I wasn't sure if I was working in the right place, doing as much with my knowledge as I would have liked, or even if I was in the right career. My personal life was changing at a pace faster than hemlines and hairstyles. My husband had just graduated from law school, I dreamed of starting a family, and my idea of combining my real love, writing, with what I already knew and liked, my legal assisting career, starting seeping into my thoughts until my brainstorm became a cascading waterfall, totally consuming my everyday life. I thought that writing about my career in a journal-type fashion would lead me to my next step in life.

It did. This book is my next step—my "follow your dream" step.

In the process of scribing my thoughts and experiences, I realized that instead of simply helping myself, what I actually sought was to reach out to other legal assistants, to those contemplating the career or even to those who were simply interested and wanted a bit of a peek into our work. I even yearned for veteran legal assistants to read these words to get a sense of community and shared understandings. I wished for readers to feel as if their best friend were giving them authentic, honest advice and the real "scoop." I hope this book reaches out and grabs all of you and perhaps even entertains you in the process.

We'll take a sometimes witty and sharp look at working with lawyers— sometimes it is extremely difficult!—and find out about the people we meet and the things we do as legal assistants.

Here, you will find out what being a legal assistant is really like. Maybe your new career as a legal assistant will be *your* "follow your dream" step.

II. Diving right to the inside to get a real-life glimpse about the world of legal assistants and their work, I shall relay an exchange that occurred in the not too distant past.

I was speaking to a student acquaintance of mine, Ruthie, who had just recently begun a legal assisting program at a local community college, and knowing I had over a decade of experience in the field, she wanted to know what being a legal assistant was *really* like. Ruthie had heard stories, both positive and negative, and wanted the inside skinny on working for those intellectual, glamorous, dramatically dynamic attorneys she'd heard so much about. Not interested in vague statements such as "you'll help attorneys do whatever they need," she wanted to know if her view was realistic and what she might be doing on a typical day. She also asked the all-important, "what are attorneys like to work for?"

Ruthie provided me with an "ideal" scenario of what she *really* thought the work was all about and her version was complete with many rich, specific details, including her thoughts about what a typical day at the office could be. Her viewpoint, and my response, went something like the following exchange, of course with quite a bit of humorous and literary license:

ME: "So, I think it's great that you want to get into this field! Tell me, what do you think it's truly like? What do you think about the work you will actually be doing?"

RUTHIE: "Well, I want to assist lawyers, and research heavy, constitutional issues."

*Ruthie's vision, which clearly forms in a bubble above her head, includes the dark-wood, brainy quietness of a posh high-profile law firm library. Very methodical, she described wearing crisp, well-tailored suits and nice shoes (men and women legal assistants).*

RUTHIE: "I will be efficient and speak eloquently in stilted legalese to my boss, as I remind him of the hearing he must attend after his lunch at the members only aristocratic club. He would politely thank me."

"Then I'll go back to my office or cubicle that is nice, neat and organized, sit down and work at a steady, but not panicky, pace, maybe writing a memo to my boss about the research I just competed. I will then go to lunch with my co-workers who are equally professional, organized and helpful. After lunch, I will pass the afternoon drafting a letter, occasionally gazing out the window at the passersby below and think, "This job is pretty cool.""

*I, being the legal assisting veteran du jour, think, then speak, MY reality conceptualizing in a large, chaotic bubble above my head:*

ME: "I do, in fact, assist lawyers, researching how to build a case out of a client who ate a piece of rubber in his burrito, or who slipped on a leaf of wet and rotting lettuce in the produce department of the grocery store, albeit in the bright, brainy chaos of a plaintiff's law firm. I wear suits and shoes. Pants when I know I will be lifting boxes during a big trial. I yell across the hall to the boss, "You've got court in 7 minutes! Don't forget the file!" knowing full well he hasn't even eaten lunch yet either. He yells back, "Call the restaurant and tell them I'll be late! And where's the file?""

I reply, "You had it on the left side of your desk, second pile, third file down."

*It helps having a memory like a central processing unit.*

"It's not here!" He barks back while he proceeds to look out the window for it.

*So much for that memory.*

It turns out the file was in the trunk of his car—he took it home last night to review it but forgot he left it in there—usually a serious no-no, but a stark reality of a volume personal injury practice just the same.

Even though I was supposed to meet my husband for lunch today, I am swamped and don't have the time, so I scarf down a bologna sandwich with Rita in the mailroom. After lunch, I pass the afternoon in a frenzied pace of phone calls, scheduling, typing letters, drafting a court paper and scanning medical records, occasionally gazing out the window at the passersby below and think, "This job is pretty cool."

*[END SCENE]*

As I shrewdly, yet truthfully explained to the protégée I was speaking with, the point of that "scene" is, Legal Assisting is a *great* profession no matter *how* you look at it, and no matter what type of environment you may find yourself in. Whether you work for a large, posh law firm with a very manageable work pace, or a busy, volume-oriented workplace with frenetic speed, both can be fun, interesting and meaningful.

The work of a paralegal is undeniably interesting, challenging and has the element of "high stakes." One can make a very exciting, distinguished career of it.

I personally think that the best part about the field is helping people at and through very crucial and stressful times in their lives.

I genuinely enjoy and respect the entire legal assisting profession, having been a part of it for over a decade. In that span of time, I have observed massive growth and the ever-increasing utilization of legal assistants; that is, more and more law firms, corporations and government agencies are using legal assistants to work their cases and settle and close deals. It is now a very solid, stable, and respected profession. It hasn't always been this way, however.

In the United States of America, the meteoric rise of legal assisting as a profession and not just a happenstance began in the 1970s and 1980s, though non-lawyers appearing and, sometimes, representing themselves and others in a court of law dates back to our colonial times, when our country and our justice system were just beginning to flesh themselves out, albeit with a heavy reliance on English "common law," that is, the laws that have flowed from several hundreds of years of English traditional laws, usually uncodified in rule or statute.

An aspiring "legal eagle" did not require formal training to become a lawyer back in the days of this country's infancy. In fact, most of the lawyers of old were really farmers who just happened to know and practice some law. This short list of farmers *cum* lawyers included fathers of our country, James Madison and Thomas Jefferson.

Some communities in the era of Colonial America, scorned or proscribed the use of lawyers, preferring to settle disputes within their communities. People were more self-sufficient then, and most of the time, these *de facto* mediations and ultimate resolutions were influenced and settled by the church, one of the more central forces in our blossoming colonial society.

Later, during the Revolutionary War, you could have counted John Adams, Aaron Burr, Patrick Henry and Alexander Hamilton among the members of the legal profession. But people still did not completely rely on lawyers for their legal problems. Colonial and early American peoples also were not as litigious as they seem today, as their lives were focused mostly on survival and solving the day-to-day problems they were faced with rather than monetary gains or teaching the big corporations a lesson.

It was not until much later, when a well-established America churning with industry and commerce, that the general population began to have access to and utilize lawyers like they do today. Lawyers frequently used legal secretaries back then, but legal assistants began to come into more prominence, taking an ever more and more important role in helping the attorney handle his or her affairs.

During the psychedelic, daisies-in-the-hair 1960s, the paralegal profession was formally established, with paralegals utilized assisting attorneys, corporations, and public agencies much more commonly and regularly than in the past. Recognition was swift in the legal industry in realizing the benefits of paralegals performing work once done almost exclusively by attorneys. This increased availability of legal services to the public and reduced legal expenses. It also freed up time for lawyers to take on more work, and further delegate that work to their paralegals. As paralegals began to bill their time on cases, they made their firms and attorneys more and more money, thus enhancing the bottom line of their respective law firms. In other words, the legal profession found that paralegals were well worth it—a valid, noble, and necessary function satisfied.

During the avocado-hued, bell-bottomed 1970s, as more and more people chose this sparking path as a career, a few independent paralegal and typing businesses cropped up in various communities, touting legal form preparation. By the time the booming 1980s reared its head, Florida, California and several other states boasted roughly 100 independent paralegal establishments, offering varied and necessary services, from simplified divorces, bankruptcies, name changes, wills, and others. Also, by this time, Legal Assisting and Paralegal programs were being planned and implemented at community colleges, universities and local technical schools. Some individuals who previously had worked as legal secretaries and who gained the appropriate knowledge moved up in the profession and became paralegals.

There is no question that this distinct career choice within the legal field began to flourish. Law firms hired more and more specially educated legal assistants and began developing them in new, creative ways, in an effort to maximize the efficiency and the productivity of staff attorneys.

Today, along with paralegals working in government, law firms, corporations and other agencies, independent paralegal services have opened across the country, and still perform such tasks as simple uncontested divorces, bankruptcy, name change, wills, certain real estate documents, and general form preparation. Lawyers themselves even use these independent legal assisting services for routine and overflow work, and to farm out tasks they can then pass on charges for to their clients. When run with the proper balance of management and ethics, never bordering on practicing law without a license, independent paralegal services are an immensely helpful tool to the general public and legal communities of our country.

These days, of course, the profession for all legal assistants, independent or otherwise, is booming and shows no sign of decrease. In fact, figures of late show that the legal assisting vocation is on track to grow faster than the average career, although competition for solid jobs is increasing due to the large number of graduates of legal assistant programs.

There are over 850,000 legal professionals in the United States today. This enormous figure includes attorneys, legal assistants, legal secretaries, runners, administrators, and legal bookkeepers. In the year 2000, legal assistants alone held approximately 188,000 positions, and enjoyed average annual salaries, dependent on community standards, of approximately $30-$45,000. Even these tidy salaries are increasing rapidly in most areas—in some of the larger metropolitan areas, veteran legal assistants or certified legal assistants can make upwards of $50,000 per year and skywards. Additionally, benefits packages abound in the legal field, including profit sharing, retirement plans, health insurance, and bonuses, which can add an additional several thousand dollars of value to the paralegal employee. According to the U.S. Department of Labor, there is a projected 63% increase of workers in the field of paralegalism—much higher than most other professions and fields.

There also is a growing trend for paralegals abroad, especially in the United Kingdom. What was once the work of junior solicitors (what they call attorneys in England) and associates, is now becoming *de rigueur* for paralegals in Europe. Though presently our U.K. counterparts do not yet share in the prestige and vast acceptance and growth of this profession, the conditions are ripe for a change in the near future, especially with the unification of the European Union community. Paralegals can also be found in Australia, Canada, Dominican Republic, and throughout Asia.

Additionally, a portion of foreign-based attorneys seeking work in the United States find that a great introduction into the American legal system can be found by attending paralegal courses and programs, and working in a law firm to gain real experience.

Indeed, wherever you are in the world, there is a place for you as a paralegal.

III. This profession has kept my own work life fast-paced and interesting and has allowed me to explore experiences I definitely would not have had if not for this choice of career.

Sometimes my days are stressful and frustrating, sometimes wonderful and fulfilling. Being a legal assistant means working hard, being extremely diligent and organized, working with different types of people and creating the best possible result for your employer and the clients you are exposed to and for whom you work by extension. It means giving something back to the world we live in and making it a better place, in oftentimes trivial and, sometimes, very big ways.

When I first set out to write this book, in addition to striving to write it to reach out to other legal assistants and those thinking about becoming one, I wrote it as if I were reading something I wish I had read when I was just starting out as a paralegal student. I longed for the true stories and real-life examples when I first began—after having dived in headfirst, I think a book such as this would have prepared me a bit better for the career I chose and some of the stark and sometimes shocking realities of the legal profession generally. Now that I, and those with whom I work and interact, consider myself a veteran in this domain, with over twelve years of know-how, I'd like to walk with you along some of my experiences at making a living in this profession. Buckle up—I'm about to take you on a ride to find out what legal assisting is *really* about.

In certain places in this book, I will use legal terminology to help illustrate a point. Some of you may already know these terms, but sometimes they will get relatively in depth, so I have created a tool to help you out. When you see this sign that reads:

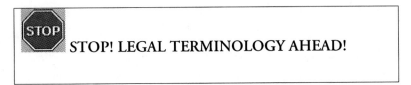

you will see an explanation of a blatantly "legalese" word coming up.

# CHAPTER II

# THE CAREER

Some may expect to walk into a law firm and be given the time and training as a paralegal. This could, and sometimes does, happen; however, in today's market, more likely than not, you will need at least some specialized education as a foundation for your paralegal career. Prospective employers will almost always opt for the individual with legal assisting training than those with none. According to the National Federation of Paralegal Associations, at least 84% of all paralegals receive some form of formal, specialized paralegal education. And what of this education?

## EDUCATION

There are many types of specialized programs in the legal assisting field. A certificate in paralegal studies may be obtained via various programs. These curricula can usually take anywhere from 6 months to 18 months, depending on the institution. An Associate in Science degree in Legal Assisting will normally take two years. There are even four-year Bachelor degree legal assistant programs, from which employers are increasingly seeking graduates. A small, but ever-growing number of individuals bring to their legal assisting career experience in another field, such as nursing or health care experience or tax and estate planning. For instance, some personal injury firms utilize paralegals with either a nursing degree or nursing background to evaluate their personal injury and medical malpractice cases. Or, criminal defense firms may try to hire paralegals who have had experience in clerical work with either the state or district attorney's office or the office of the public defender, or even law enforcement agencies.

At the dawn of the new millennium, the year 2000, approximately 2,400 formal legal assisting education and training programs were offered in the United States by various entities that include community colleges, business schools and traditional universities. Your school and course work should be accredited, to receive the maximum benefit and flexibility for your career, and courses should typically cover legal terminology, ethics, legal and technical writing, and areas of substantive law, such as bankruptcy, real estate, family law, criminal law, and civil litigation skills, as well as electives depending on the individual's needs and/or desired track. Most of these schools also offer some sort of placement or job assistance service to its students through their career or alumni services departments.

A great resource for finding a paralegal school or program in your area is the U.S. Department of Labor Bureau of Labor Statistics website. This site also has a wealth of up-to-date information on salaries, job outlooks, general information and useful links. Specifically, you can log on to www.bls.gov/oco, for the occupational outlook of certain professions. Browse through the Professional and Related Occupations and scroll down to "Legal" where you will find Paralegals and Legal Assistants listed. This is a great source for obtaining additional informative background on the paralegal field.

Additionally, using any of the various search engines on the Internet, you may find a variety of listings for paralegal schools by searching for "paralegals and schools" or "list of paralegal schools" or the like.

A few sites you may find advantageous, and which catalogue and direct you to schools that offer paralegal programs, follow.

http://www.allparalegalschools.com
http://www.careerschooldirectory./com/pages/adminsec/paralegal.htm
http://www.education-online-search.com/legal_training/paralegal_ school /paralegal school.shtml
http://www.searchforcolleges.net/Legal-and-Paralegal-Programs.htm
http://www.career-education.info/paralegal-programs.htm

However, most of these sites do not mention community colleges, so don't forget to check the institutions in your state or city for possible paralegal programs.

If you would like to move further in the career, you may voluntarily take the Certified Legal Assistant (CLA) exam. To take this exam, you must have certain standards such as a specified amount of education and/or experience. Then, three times a year, you may sit for a 2-day examination. Those who pass earn the designation, Certified Legal Assistant. The CLA designation is administered through the National Association of Legal Assistants (NALA). Also, like attorneys who specialize in certain areas of law, the paralegal may also specialize in an area of law by taking a Certified Legal Assistant Specialist (CLAS) exam in certain substantive law areas. To learn more about these prestigious designations, you may contact the National Association of Legal Assistants at www.nala.org. This organization also publishes a magazine, *Facts & Findings*, also found on their website, and is a wealth of information relating to paralegalism that the current or prospective paralegal can use to his or her benefit.

In addition to the CLA credential, there is another available qualification, that of Registered Paralegal (RP). The National Federation of Paralegal Associations administers this particular test and again, there are certain educational and/or experience requirements to sit for the exam. You may contact The National Federation of Paralegal Associations at www.nfpa.org. *The National Paralegal Reporter* is this organization's magazine and is also a useful cornucopia of information. Some of the regional paralegal associations also publish newsletters and other publications for your information. These can usually be found on the Internet or by contacting each respective organization for further information.

Another trade publication of interest to anyone either in the paralegal profession or thinking of becoming a paralegal is *Legal Assistant Today* magazine, which has articles and features relating to every aspect of the field of legal assisting. *Legal Assistant Today* magazine also has a plethora of information available through their website www.legalassistanttoday.com.

My own paralegal schooling was nothing less than indispensable, illuminating, and fantastically interesting. I attended my local community college and earned an Associate in Science (A.S.) degree in Legal Assisting. As I found out through my years as a legal assistant/paralegal, the course work required for this degree proved a great foundation for what lay ahead, and went a long way to preparing me for most of the trials (no pun intended!) and tribulations of working within the legal community. I highly recommend obtaining a formal education prior to or during your foray into this field. I do know of legal assistants who were simply hired, learned on-the-job and ended up being excellent, conscientious, and hard-working employees; however, comprehensive legal knowledge, issue-spotting skills, and general understanding of law and procedure flows directly from the training you receive, whether in a degree-seeking program, or on-the-job. A solid curriculum of classes geared towards preparing you for a career in this field is an invaluable tool—both to you *and* your employer.

As part of my drive to become a successful and commercially desirable paralegal, I took and passed the aforementioned CLA exam shortly after I graduated with my degree.

During my own schooling, I was fortunate to take classes that taught discipline in legal terminology, legal writing, researching, issue spotting, aspects of certain areas of substantive law (criminal, bankruptcy, real estate, etc.), as well as typing, office and file management, and document organization and management.

Comprehending legal terminology, what the terms really mean and how to apply them properly, is an extensive and integral part of the focus of a successful paralegal schooling program. Words and concepts such as "discovery," "interrogatories," "motions in limine," "arbitration," "guardianship," and "scintilla" will, with time and experience, become second nature. *Black's Law Dictionary*, published by West Publishing Company, will, at least early on, become an intimate partner of yours.

Learning to write in the fashion that lawyers and judges expect to see things written is a vital and considerable segment of any legal assisting curriculum. This stilted and sometimes archaic sounding language is sometimes referred to as "legalese." Interpreting the law and applying it to a particular case or fact scenario is a tool that every lawyer, judge or legal professional will expect from a paralegal. Also, you will learn that the legal field and the practice of law, as well as paralegalism, is not really *what* you know, although it is good to have a vast storehouse of knowledge and experience from which to draw, but rather knowing *where* to look to find your answers. No attorney out there knows the answer to every legal question that may be posed—but I'll bet dollars to doughnuts that he or she has the tools to find an answer somewhere, be it a colleague practicing in an area the attorney does not, an online research service or a reference book. It can be the same with experienced paralegals—they add value to the attorney(s) for whom they work by being trained and yet versatile enough to find a solution to what the attorney is asking them to do.

You will learn about many research tools and reference books, such as the Reporters, which are the books where appellate cases are reported, becoming the basis for case law, which is how statutes and rules are interpreted, and how and what to look for in those books.

 **STOP! LEGAL TERMINOLOGY AHEAD!**

"Appellate": relating to a case that has already been decided at the trial level, which is now "on appeal." One or both of the parties disagree with the trial court, and thus appeal the case to an appellate court for further ruling or based on an alleged error of the trial court. All Reporters contain only appellate rulings; due to the vast number of cases and lawsuits filed, trial level proceedings are not reported on in any Reporter.

A solid education will be one of your greatest allies in this field. It will be what guns and horses were to the Spaniards in their conquest at ancient Cajamarca—the combination of preparedness, strategy and the best equipment and training, which could be the deciding line between victory and defeat and horrendous loss of life. Superb legal assistants can "see the forest through the trees," make judgment calls on the fly, and possess the skills to make their attorneys more productive and successful; education serves as their compass and trail map.

However, despite all the groundwork laid by school training, there really is nothing that can teach you the real-life skills and experience other than working in a law firm or other law-related entity and receiving on-the-job education. It is one thing to strategize battle plans in camp and quite another to implement them in the unforgiving fields. You must be able to excel both in your studies *and* out in the real world.

## FINDING A PARALEGAL POSITION

If you are interested in taking your legal assisting or paralegal education out of the classroom and into the realm of lawyers and law firms, you will go through the trials of finding your first (or second, third, seventeenth…) paralegal position. I have found much luck through staffing agencies specializing in the legal field, as they are plugged into the specific, immediate needs of the legal community. Also, local bar associations usually have placement services available for paralegals, as well as attorneys, bookkeepers, runners and other legal staff. Other, more traditional means of finding a job are classified ads, internet job postings, word of mouth, or simply contacting firms that you are interested in and inquiring as to their hiring needs. A great resume is crucial to getting noticed and hired. Print out your resume on professional paper, and lay it out nicely and coherently, with education, work experience, other special skills such as typing speed and word processing proficiency, and references neatly outlined. Be sure to include your contact information: name, address, phone number, e-mail address, etc. A professional, concise cover letter along with the resume should serve as an introduction to your education, experiences, work ethics and skills. There are many references in books, or on the web relating to drafting spectacular resumes and cover letters, and if need be, scan a few of these to punctuate your key points on paper.

When you get called for an interview, be equipped to go at a moment's notice in order to capitalize on the opportunity. Have your interview suit at the ready, pressed crisply and ironed, an extra copy of your resume on hand, and try to sneak a peek at the firm granting you the interview—find out what area of law they practice, where they are located, and have some background and a couple of questions ready to ask. For example, if the firm you are to interview with is a medical mal-practice firm, perhaps be prepared to discuss some the recent findings regarding drugs that show horrible, unintended side effects that sometimes kill people. Or, if the firm practices products liability law, bring up automaker liability for burst tire incidents, or the dangerous nature of certain products. These inquiries may seem unnecessary, but they may help to show the firm and your interviewer, who may be the attorney him or herself, that you are interested enough in the position to keep up with current events, and that you have a general interest in what the firm does. Interest, enthusiasm, and showing you did your homework will go a long way towards giving you a sure shot at an opportunity, even without experience in the beginning. And also, first impressions are huge in the legal field, so, arrive early! As my later years as an office administrator taught me, I really did take notice of who showed up early or late for their interview.

If, at first, you find it difficult in your geographical area to find a true paralegal position, other options could include starting as a receptionist, file clerk, secretary or other positions within the law firm or entity, to gain the necessary experience and contacts to, later, morph into a true paralegal position. And, as touched on later, there are more than private practice law firms with whom to seek employment—judges require staff members, as do state or district attorney's offices, the office of the public defender, and state and governmental agencies as well.

I personally know a fantastic woman who began her legal career as a receptionist for an extremely prestigious law firm and did such an impressive and professional job, that the owner and senior partner of the firm made her his personal assistant and personal paralegal within six years! I also know plenty of others, including myself, who have started as file clerks, receptionists, runners and secretaries, only to find themselves bona fide paralegals in no time.

There is certainly no harm in starting a little lower in the ranks in your career than you initially thought, so long as you keep one eye on the path you envision for yourself and strive for that higher, attainable position at all times.

## THE EARLY YEARS

As for my own first foray into the paralegal workforce, while still attending classes at my local community college, in its Associate in Science Legal Assisting program, I began working as a part-time file clerk in a predominantly family law practice, with one of the more prominent and prestigious firms in the area of family practice. I mundanely found this job through the classified ads, sent in a resume, interviewed twice and was hired. I worked approximately 20 hours per week, in the mornings, while going to school full time in the evenings.

Though I had no idea at the time, in hindsight, this particular firm was the most professional in which I had ever worked, even to this day. They had systems in place and procedures for almost every aspect of organized, capable file management, and I found out (later of course, due to experience and retrospection) that the senior attorneys and office manager had painstakingly, throughout the years, honed these procedures to a point where nothing slipped through the cracks, no deadlines were ever missed, and developed virtually fool-proof methods of advancing, calendaring and scheduling the progress of a file. Even though these procedures could be cumbersome at times, this in turn increased productivity and the bottom line of the firm—they made more money with less effort. The paralegal should not, when forging organizational ideas and procedures, forget that practicing law is indeed a business that must make continuous money for rent, phones, employees, insurance, reference materials, office furniture, and many, many other expenses.

My new employer also had a sterling reputation amongst the rest of the local legal community, to no surprise, thanks in no small part to the firm's adherence to deadline, procedure, and wholly ethical practice of law. This office is where I built the granite-solid foundation of my habits, work ethic and skills for my future paralegal career. And, this is where I learned that, until I actually knew the full measure of the work expected of me to be able to perform well on a consistent basis, my work ethic, personality and responsible habits would have to see me through.

Even as I was simply filing papers, I paid close attention to what I was filing and learned which documents were pleadings, which were correspondence and which were discovery materials. I read some motions and orders and got the feel for the format of various documents. I soon learned that even though the legal industry appears to be largely form-driven, a good and thorough legal assistant still must know the general terminology of documents, such as motions, to be able to tailor it to specific needs on whichever case upon which they are working.

STOP! LEGAL TERMINOLOGY AHEAD!

"Pleading(s)": a legal pleading is a paper or document filed with the court at certain crucial junctures, where one party 'pleads' for some specific relief. A complaint or petition for relief are always considered pleadings, as are most motions (see below). In contrast, most discovery (see below) is not considered a pleading, with a few exceptions.

"Motion(s)": Courts generally do not act on their own, with some minor exceptions. In order for a Court to properly act on something or grant requested relief, the Court must be 'moved,' that is, a Motion must be made, which is then heard by the Court and ruled upon. "Orders" then grant or deny the relief requested.

"Discovery": Differentiated from pleadings, discovery is the process by which both sides in a lawsuit 'discover' certain facts in order to help flesh out their case and their respective points of view, and is also what each item in the discovery process may come to be referred to as. Examples of kinds of discovery can include: requests for production, which is asking the other side to produce certain documents for inspection and copying; interrogatories, which are written questions that must be answered under oath; and depositions, where a person or party, the 'deponent,' are 'deposed,' or give testimonial answers to questions by the attorneys under oath as if they were on a witness stand.

I found out by simply being alert to my surroundings and the goings-on about me that there are things to be learned, to the paralegal's advantage, even when starting at the seeming bottom.

I also learned how to organize files efficiently and how and when to follow up with tasks. Different attorneys prefer their files organized in sometimes individual and particular ways, so make sure to find out early on from whomever is training you, be it office manager, other paralegal, or the attorney him or herself, to be clear on how the files are expected to be organized. In this law firm, "tasks" were divided up and each staff member was assigned a particular and individual duty or duties. For example, the firm employed a dedicated word processor who cranked out documents all day, a scheduler who scheduled hearings, depositions, client meetings, and everything else that was placed on the attorneys' calendars, a person whose job was to do nothing but make copies for whomever needed copies of documents, a runner whose task was to pick up and take filings to the courthouse and hand deliver documents or copies to other law firms, and legal assistants who were assigned to the intake of new cases, setting up files immediately, and who also worked on the bulk of the paperwork and responsibilities along with the attorneys. There were also monthly file reviews, of which I am a huge proponent.

File review is, in my opinion, and in the opinion of some of the most successful attorneys with whom I have had the pleasure of working, one of the most crucial and necessary tasks a law firm, by and through its paralegal staff, should undertake. It is difficult, if not impossible, to remember everything that must be done, especially deadlines, accurately on each file. Things to do, left by the wayside, most notably in a high volume practice such as personal injury or medical malpractice, can have a tendency to slip through the cracks. Weeks turn into months, months into years. Even if your firm does not have a formal file review method in place, I recommend you formulate one on your own initiative, even if you perform yours only quarterly or twice a year. I believe a file review should be done at least every six months; that way, especially if you work in the area of civil litigation, you will not run into the potential danger of having a case dismissed due to non-activity, or more egregiously, miss a statute of limitations. Of course, if you are involved with criminal defense work, the deadlines are much tighter for speedy trial purposes, which deadlines you will learn in your particular jurisdiction. The ability to catch mistakes or a potentially case-killing error before it happens, by instituting procedural safeguards, will make your attorney happy he hired you, and your job that much easier.

STOP! LEGAL TERMINOLOGY AHEAD!

"Statute of Limitations": each state has what are called statutes of repose or limitations. They simply limit the length of time from an injury or damage that a lawsuit may be brought, in the interests of judicial economy and of the freshness of evidence.

"Speedy Trial": In criminal law matters, a Defendant (the one charged with a crime) has a right to be brought to trial in a speedy manner, usually in a certain number of months, so that he or she does not potentially languish in jail or on pre-trial house arrest awaiting trial for several years. Can vary by classification of crime (felony, misdemeanor, etc.).

I conducted a file review every calendar quarter during my later years at other jobs, without being prompted to do so by others, including attorneys. However, recognizing the need for file review and the value and convenience it can bring to the paralegal's tasks, I created a list of every case's date of last correspondence, last pleading filed, outstanding discovery, a "to-do" list, and any questions to ask my attorney. I also made notes such as, "Calendar to follow up in 30 days." Believe me, this conscientious attention to detail saved a lot of potential disasters from happening. If you catch things from happening, *before* they happen, you are immensely more valuable to your attorney, your firm and its clients.

Of course, I didn't want to stay a file clerk for long, and there is only so much you can learn from glancing at documents as you file them. When I finally graduated with my Associate in Science degree in Legal Assisting, the office manager called me in and explained that they had actually created a position for me, Junior Legal Assistant! I was so excited and began to work full-time immediately. I was out of school and finally working full time as a paralegal in my new career! I was elated. And I was to learn an overwhelming lot of information and life lessons.

In my new position, at first, I mostly helped the senior legal assistants organize their cases and created a veritable ton of trial notebooks. Organization of files is crucial, no matter what type of case you work on. What good is critical information if you can't find it?

**STOP! LEGAL TERMINOLOGY AHEAD!**

"Trial Notebook": going to trial means that a case comes to its head, its boiling point—all the facts, allegations, evidence, witnesses, and arguments of the attorneys will be heard at trial in this forum. A trial notebook organizes the main issues, evidence, and can contain outlines, opening and/or closing arguments, jury instructions, or whatever else the attorney likes to have at his or her fingertips at trial.

Trial notebooks are very popular in litigation practice. They contain pertinent correspondence and pleadings, discovery, witness and exhibit lists, evidentiary documents, and attorney notes, which are tabbed and indexed. I recall also making special deposition notebooks, wherein I copied all pertinent depositions, placed them into a binder and indexed and tabbed them to make them easily accessible. These days, some law firms are turning to computerized technologies such as scanning of documents and exhibits, but whether on paper or computer, the basics of organizing a case remain the same.

In my new position, I also created new forms and re-worked old ones, drafted letters and motions, and other documents. I also assisted the attorneys in tasks they needed done, including copying, running to the courthouse to file papers, whatever they might need. I even helped the scheduling secretary once or twice. Working with her, even for this brief period of time, would be the beginning of why I feel that scheduling can be one of the most dreaded tasks facing a paralegal, which is and has often been borne out by other legal assistant acquaintances of mine. Imagine getting four or five lawyers (maybe there are four defendants in the lawsuit!), a court reporter and the deponent (person being deposed in a deposition), who just might happen to be a surgeon with a schedule that would make lawyers sweat, all at the same location at the same time. Organizing these multi varied schedules can be a herculean task. Sound easy? Sometimes it isn't! But it happens every hour of every business day in the life of a paralegal somewhere.

I learned that in scheduling anything, no matter how experienced you are and how insignificant it may seem, you must consciously think about: 1) who is going; 2) why are they going; 3) who has to know about it; and 4) who gets properly noticed, copied and/or subpoenaed? And even though some jurisdictions do not require coordinating, that is, calling the opposing party and actually going through your calendars to pick a date and time good for both, I highly recommend it. This process is courteous and saves time with rescheduling, and will give your firm and attorney an ethical appearance, which can work to his or her advantage at a time when your attorney needs some leniency. Noticing means filing an original notice of deposition or notice of hearing (or whatever you are scheduling) with the clerk of court and mailing copies to all parties involved, such as opposing counsel(s), court reporters, and judicial assistants. To subpoena someone or something (i.e., medical records), you must prepare the subpoena, have it issued by the clerk or attorney, and usually, personally served upon the "someone" or "something."

Inevitably some of what you schedule will need to be canceled and/or rescheduled. You must then go through the process of notifying all involved about the cancellation and then rescheduling; essentially, performing the whole process over again. Coordination of events from the outset helps minimize this wearisome procedure.

My position at the family law firm was fantastic, and provided me with the first-hand groundwork I needed to become a more resourceful, independent paralegal, and helped me to instill confidence in my abilities. It was so enjoyable to have such a conducive learning environment that I was fired up each and every day, and literally threw myself into the work. I remained diligent, kept organized, asked pertinent questions, and did not miss any deadlines. If I even had an inkling that I couldn't get a task done in time, I would immediately inform the assigning attorney or supervisor in order to better delegate and solve the potential problem. There is no shame, and I felt none, whatsoever in letting your attorney know that you may need assistance on certain tasks, especially the closer and closer you get to trial.

Additionally, I learned a number of handy tools to help me keep, organize, and retrieve information on expert witnesses, court reporters, process servers, trial exhibit services, and other resources that law firms use frequently. The family law firm kept a notebook of these businesses and people, but some firms use some form of a computerized index or case management software, or even a good old-fashioned Rolodex. Whatever you use, paper or technological, make sure the information is in a common place where everyone can use it, that everyone *knows* how to use it, and keep it up to date with phone numbers, addresses, etc.

I also learned the professional ins and outs of how, when and why to interact with the legal assistants, attorneys, office manager and clients. I learned through time and experience, as this is really the best way, in my opinion, when to go to an attorney for a problem (legal advice or issue), when to seek out another legal assistant (pretty much everything else!) or when to involve the office manager (health insurance, personnel issues, etc.).

Flowing necessarily from my interaction with attorneys and other legal support staff, I was also to gain intimate knowledge of a tremendously important skill that each paralegal should at the very least attempt to master—human relations and working with different types of personalities.

There were a couple of staff members, who, while very nice, didn't have the spark and energy that I thought everyone had. I surmised that everyone was like me—driven, but not arrogant or ruthless—energetic, and motivated to do as good a job as I possibly could. I was extremely idealistic and naive. If *I* could do it, why couldn't everyone else do the things I was doing as well?!? That was my mantra and has been the source of some of my greatest frustrations in the legal field. I was my own worst enemy in my realism, not fully appreciating that not every individual wanted to or could attain such a high level of skill, proficiency, and efficiency, which were all hallmarks of my high standards. I agonized over why it was this way for some persons and wished that people would change, or, in the alternative, that I could show people better ways to complete tasks that might motivate them and make them see the fun in being a paralegal or legal support member, as well as the advantages and financial success they would enjoy in the job market if they used some of the tools of which I speak.

I will never forget a regular staff meeting one day when a particular employee, who I thought was already lackadaisical about his work, complained that he had too much to do and couldn't finish it all—ever! That resulted in the senior attorneys "re-working" his workload and giving some of it to me! Although I knew enough to keep my mouth shut, inside, I was outraged. To me, the additional amount or volume of work that was being heaped onto my plate was not the problem—I knew I could handle more. It was the simple fact that this person was complaining about not being able to do his job but yet really didn't exert himself in his tasks in a day-to-day setting. It wasn't like this person was saying that the firm had gotten generally busier, and that therefore his duties were more than the other employees, or that it was just a really tight time with trials and all— not at all. He just didn't want as much work as he was given, an opinion borne solely from his overall lethargy and sloth. And yet, here he sat during this meeting, not being held accountable for his actions, which I thought were plain for all to see, including the attorneys and firm administrator. This gentleman was perpetually late, called in sick often, and still was allowed to behave in this manner! I felt like crying right there in the blue and white conference room, I could hardly believe it.

This was one of many lessons I was to learn about some individuals comprising the workforce in the legal community, which I imagine is probably also consistent with a cross-section of employees in many other occupations. Not everyone is treated the same and not everything is fair. And sometimes, what may be important to you, may not be important to the management. In some cases, management would rather work with someone already in place, than to take the time and effort to seek out, hire and train another person. There are always going to be people who are under your standards, at your standards and above your standards, and you have to learn to deal with all of them.

This was a turning point for me. My vision of the well-oiled workplace of fairness, justice and efficiency was irreparably tarnished by that moment, a victim of my high standards. Looking back, it is still my opinion that this firm is one of the most professional with whom I had ever worked, and I learned valuable skills and tools there, but even then, it wasn't perfect—nothing is.

However, at this time in my career, as naivete wore off and reality dug its nails in, I was also growing restless and desired to be a legal assistant on my own—not just assisting other legal assistants. I had also just recently taken and passed the CLA exam. It was a difficult test, but months of studying got me through and I had passed it on the first try! I was on top of the world! When I opened the envelope containing my test results, I was thrilled when I saw, "Congratulations..." I was now a Certified Legal Assistant, and an almost inexplicable feeling fills you when you sign your name, and then add a professional designation such as "CLA" after it. I remember typing memos upon memos with my name and new title in all capital letters and confirming things, no matter how minimal or insignificant, in letters, just so that I could sign my name with "CLA" after it! I felt immediate stature and confidence when I earned my CLA designation and I feel this accomplishment did, in the long run, get me better-quality jobs and more attractive salaries.

Still a Junior Legal Assistant, I felt I had gained enough knowledge to work on my own and sustain myself, solo, in a law firm and report directly to attorneys. So, after another month or so, after I thoroughly thought things through, I gave my proper two-week notice and started looking for a position as a legal assistant. Unfortunately, the family law firm I was with did not have an opening for a full-fledged legal assistant and weren't planning to expand. So, in order to find what I was looking for, I had to seek it elsewhere.

When I left, my boss told me I would make a great lawyer and asked if I had ever considered going to law school. I had, actually, thought about this, but it would remain in the depths of my thoughts, even to this day. I suppose I just never had such a burning desire to be a lawyer, a champion of justice, a litigator—none of this seemed to appeal to me. I was fully satisfied being a legal assistant, a valid and satisfying career in its own right. (In contrast, I've always passionately ached to be a writer, which is why I constantly tried to squeeze time at night and on weekends to put pen to paper!)

Anyway, after I left that first real law office job, it was at this juncture that I started my journey into seedy offices behind railroad tracks, dysfunctional technophobes, and attorneys who bounced paychecks.

From my posh, professional first-job environment, I landed in an old, dank office with a firm who practiced mostly insurance defense. The dank came because the offices were located in a smoking building and the firm allowed smoking on the job, which several employees partook of. The attorneys and staff in this firm were older, the next youngest after me being in their late forties. The five women who already worked for the firm were so old-fashioned and stodgy, I didn't even know what to talk about with them. I was about 24 years old at this time. They even still had typewriters and rotary phones! In 1995! To make matters worse, my boss, a very sweet man and good attorney, was very sickly and either took naps for much of the day or simply would not come to work. I was bored out of my skull! I couldn't stand it—eight hours of doing essentially nothing is a dreary, very long day to deal with. I would maybe type a letter or two a day. I would file perhaps three pieces of paper and then…nothing. I felt I had to look busy, but it was torture not knowing what was expected of me. I even asked point-blank what to do, or what I should be doing and they just told me to do "whatever my attorney needed." The other attorneys and their support staff didn't seem to know or even care what I did throughout the day. I kept somewhat alert by organizing the heck out of the fifty or so files my attorney was assigned to handle. I mean, when I say there wasn't a single piece of paper out of place in my files, I mean it! But there was nothing else to do and I dreaded going into work every day just to be bored to tears for eight hours.

This got my gears working, and I came to a startling realization: the individual paralegal should be careful to not just take any employment that comes along, but to think about their personality type, what are their general likes and dislikes, and use these factors to help determine the best area of law suited for that individual's needs.

My early legal assisting positions taught me a lot about what type of law firm and type of law to choose. I learned that for myself, I wanted to seek out litigation-type fast-paced work. I needed challenge and to keep busy. Luckily for my bored existence, my boss retired after almost a year and I began my job search again.

This time, I was led into a law firm in a downtown high rise who hired me on the spot. It was a beautiful office with great views of the city, but unfortunately, after only a couple of weeks, the attorney, whom I came to find out was really mean-spirited, began paying me late and then, bounced my paycheck! He didn't even acknowledge the fact that he couldn't actually afford a legal assistant, but had hired me anyway and was actually angry with *me* when I inquired of him about it. It was morning, about 11:00 a.m., when he finally rolled into the office, and I told him I had been at the bank that morning and they had said my paycheck could not be cashed. I very nicely asked him about it, thinking it may have been a banking error.

Well, after he yelled at me for an hour about him working so hard just to have his wife "kept" and his girlfriends "happy," I simply walked out of that job, which is a first for me, as I had always given proper notice in the past when leaving an employer. I just walked out. Somehow, my fight or flight instinct kicked in and screamed at me, "Flight!" Something clicked in me to just leave because I could tell that this situation was *never* going to work out. The attorney ran down the hall, first begging me to stay, saying I was a great worker, then screaming that he would, "Dock me for the rest of the day!" Ha! He was threatening not to pay me? Gee, he's not paying me anyway! I called back to him, "What else is new?" and flounced down to my car. (I know, I know, me with the oh so harsh words!) But I never heard from him again.

In retrospect, I could have contacted the Bar association about him or even the State Attorney's Office about intentionally writing a bad check, but I didn't. I just wanted to put that miserable man and his practically defunct law firm behind me and move on.

Which is exactly what I did.

After only a four-day job search, perusing the classifieds, sending out resumes, and getting the word out amongst my friends, I landed at a personal injury law firm. Right away I knew this firm would be different and I felt like I would be here for a long time. (There is a lot to be said about trusting your instincts in this profession!) The office was nice, elegant, quiet (at least that day) and the people seemed nice. When my soon-to-be boss interviewed me, he confessed that he had never had a CLA work for him before and was excited about that. We clicked right away and I was hired at a solid, high-end salary, plus an array of very good benefits.

Here is where I really feel I started to shine as a legal assistant. I was given so much responsibility and such a high volume of work that I felt like I was literally thrown into the fire. I remained in those raging flames for the next five years.

I was to be the legal assistant to the senior attorney/owner of the firm. He was very nice and appreciated my work right away. In fact, my first week there I received a $100 bonus just because he, "could tell I was different." I didn't think I was doing anything special—just doing my job, conscientious, organized, as I had been taught. But, as I had already learned, and it was confirmed here in my new workplace, people were different and they didn't all have the same standards. If yours are high, and you consistently meet them, you *will* stand out.

My first day at this firm, I was given the filing to catch up on. What a mound! There had to be thousands of pieces of paper in that filing pile! So, after being introduced to everyone, which at the time was a staff of five, I went to the back of the office and dug into the filing. First, I sorted the filing alphabetically. Then, I started with the A's. It went surprisingly fast. I caught a glimpse of their filing system—separate folders for each deposition, medical provider, etc., and created labels and folders for those documents that needed them.

By noon, I was at the "T's." My boss and the office manager thought it would have taken me at least a few days, even a couple of weeks, to complete this horrible glut of filing. I think my boss was impressed that I simply got to work, took initiative and remained there until the job was complete. I didn't stop to eat, drink, or take breaks.

At noon that first day, my boss treated me to a burger and fries for lunch. The whole staff sat around the conference room table eating lunch.

"Well," I thought, "This is like a family." They all chatted about the cases and their lives.

"What a nice place to work—I think I'll like it here." I thought.

I finished the filing my first day.

After the filing, during the first week, I was literally and actually handed the firm's entire litigation department. I was told I, "Could handle it." Yikes! I wasn't so sure, but I was determined to prove myself.

The litigation—cases in which a lawsuit had been filed—consisted of around 125 cases at the time, for which my boss was the attorney. In my experience, personal injury caseloads, per legal assistant and attorney, can vary from a low of 50 to a super high of 500, with the average being around 100-150. Any more than that and a firm usually sacrifices quality over quantity. They probably have a frazzled staff also!

The first thing I did when handed the litigation cases was make a comprehensive list of all of the files. They actually already had a list, but it was incomplete, inaccurate and outdated. Nobody had even touched it for at least the past four months. That was unacceptable to me as I thought that in order to formulate and conceptualize a game plan for organizing the firm, I had to know ALL cases that were in litigation, as opposed to cases only in the treatment phase (clients' medical treatment) or demand phases, which were not my responsibility. After all, I was now responsible for these litigation files, and knew my boss would look to me to organize them and keep them moving, under his supervision.

How could I rely solely on memory to remember cases and their statuses? Even if I could, which I can't, and is likely impossible unless one happens to have a photographic memory, why would I even want to? Not having a case list, living by the seat of one's pants, trying to remember everything in every file, sounds to me like a recipe to miss deadlines, and potentially mishandle clients' cases.

So, first, I made my list, going through the file cabinet one by one and adding cases as I went. Nobody told me to do this, they just said, "You will be responsible for the litigation files. Here's a list." I simply updated the list and added columns for mediation and trial dates and general status. This way I could also keep track of mediations and trials coming up, which are two major events in the civil litigation process of a case.

STOP! LEGAL TERMINOLOGY AHEAD!

"Mediation": to reiterate, when a case goes to trial, it means that a case comes to its head, its boiling point—all the facts, allegations, evidence, witnesses, and arguments of the attorneys will be heard at trial in this forum. However, this process can be lengthy and drawn-out, and possibly very expensive for the litigants. Several forms of Alternate Dispute Resolution (ADR) have been created to help out people in lawsuits who claim to have been damaged, but which attempt to resolve quicker and more economically than traditional litigation and trials. Mediation is one of these such alternate dispute resolutions, where a neutral third party disinterested mediator attempts to facilitate resolution by meetings with both sides, called caucusing. If an agreement is reached, the parties do not have to attend trial; their matter has been resolved by their own decision-making and the skills of the mediator. Mediation should be contrasted with arbitration, another alternate dispute resolution, as mediation is traditionally non-binding, while arbitration is usually more formal and also binding on the parties.

Next, I sorted through the work that had been on the office manager's desk for— who knows how long? It turned out to be months, in some cases. From her desk to mine went a jumble of phone messages, discovery, pleadings and correspondence.

How to organize this caseload and all of the tasks?

It took me a few tries to perfect my technique, but I finally came up with an efficient, easy to maintain, and practically foolproof method. I also enhanced a couple of ideas gleaned from my first-firm experience where everyone and every-thing seemed to be supremely organized.

I organized the work into categories. I grabbed five stackable, black plastic office trays and created labels such as "miscellaneous litigation, scheduling, dis-covery, suits to be filed, and filing." These trays were the "homes" for my work.

When the mail came in every day or someone gave me a memo or a task to do, I would put it in my separate, wire "in-box" prior to my looking at it. I acted as my own "filter" for my work. Usually I looked through my in-box and sorted the mail or tasks to do immediately. If not, I knew it would be in my in-box until I did, instead of having the potential of being lost in the shuffle of other papers or piles.

From the in-box, it went, or "filtered", through me. If I saw a notice of hearing, it went in my scheduling tray to be calendared and to notify our client, if need be. Same with a notice of taking deposition, where I would, when going through my scheduling tray, automatically calendar the deposition and do a form letter to our client (if it was our client's deposition) informing them of the date, time and location.

To complete this process, say, after the attorney signed the letter informing a client of a deposition, I would create a separate deposition manila file for that particular deponent in that specific case, which would then be waiting for the attorney when he attended the deposition, and would be easy for him to find.

Correspondence that needed to be acted on would go into my miscellaneous tray, as would other pleadings such as production from non-party, and motions to review.

Discovery materials such as interrogatories, admissions and requests for production would go into the discovery tray to either be reviewed or responded to.

Likewise, if my boss asked me to set a hearing, I pulled out a copy of a scheduling form I had custom-created for myself, and wrote down the case name, what I was scheduling, and any pertinent information such as deadlines and placed it in my scheduling tray to do later.

If my boss asked me to prepare a complaint and all pertinent paperwork to go with it, I would jot the information down on a "Notes" form, and stick it in my "discovery/suits to be filed" tray. I would then get to it at a later time, but still in a timely manner.

This was the easiest way to organize; however, every lawyer and law firm is different. They may already have a system in place and will expect you to use it. But, here, there was no system and every file seemed to be set up differently. Uniformity, I learned, is critical. Whatever you do on one file, do on every file, at least of that type. For example, all medical malpractice cases in your office should be set up the same, perhaps with the same colors or labels, and the same sub-files such as medical records, expert opinions, attorney notes, research, etc. Consistency is key for finding items quickly.

This system worked well not only for me, but if I wasn't there for some reason, whoever was could easily find what they were looking for on my desk. It was easy and wasn't so hyper-organized that the system took up a lot of needless time.

The result was that I always had the answers at the ready. If my boss asked, "What's the status of scheduling those depositions?" I would pull out my notes in my scheduling tray. My note for that particular case would state the date the task was given to me, and a place to write down activity, such as, "2/4/02 @ 11:45 a.m., left message for secretary—will check with their client and call back by Wednesday." It's a great idea to have your own personal abbreviations for frequently used words and phrases. For example, for the above note, I would have written, "2/4/02 @ 11:45—LM for OC (opposing counsel, see below) sec (secretary or assistant) re: will chk w/cl (client) and CB (call back) by Wed." This way, you don't have to write everything out thereby, over the long haul, being more economical with your time.

 **STOP! LEGAL TERMINOLOGY AHEAD!**

Well, not exactly legal terminology, but some helpful and common abbreviations used in the legal field and elsewhere:

LM: Left Message
OC or OPC: Opposing Counsel
W/: "with" whatever follows
W/O: Without
B/W: Between
B/C: Because
K: Contract
DOM: Dissolution of Marriage
PAT: Paternity matters
TPR: Termination of Parental Rights Cases
PI: Personal Injury
CB: Call Back
JA: Judicial Assistant
CT or CR: Courtroom Number
Δ: Defendant or Respondent
Π: Plaintiff or Petitioner
MTN: Motion
NOH: Notice of Hearing
NOCOH: Notice of Cancellation of Hearing
SOP: Service of Process
MED/DIV: Mediation and Diversion Services (differs by jurisdiction)
MEDMAL: Medical Malpractice

My system would also alleviate having big, bulky files piled in various places all over my desk. Thick files stuffed with all sorts of legal pleadings, papers, medical records, and correspondence strewn all about the office always overwhelmed me. Looking at an organized work area always energized and inspired me, and left me with a sense of accomplishment. There was no need for an entire file if I was just scheduling depositions. If I couldn't get to a task right away, I would place my form/notes into my scheduling tray for later.

My boss was very impressed with this simple, but efficient system. But more importantly, it worked for me. I saw everything that came "through" me and sorted everything appropriately.

I could also visually look and see if I was caught up on my work and where I was getting backed up. I always knew exactly what work was on my desk and what I had to do.

This system, or a similar version, can be used no matter what area of law you are in. Just changing the labels on the trays to appropriate tasks will suffice. For instance, usually, most legal assistants have to schedule, be it a deposition, a hearing, or a real estate closing. If you are doing real estate, you may additionally categorize by title searches and closings. Also, one does not necessarily have to use trays—I just found them sturdy and neat. You may use file folders, baskets or even shelves. As long as you organize your work where you don't have a big jumble of papers on your desk and your work is organized in some logical fashion, you should be on top of your workload.

Planning your day and your work is also time-efficient and critical.

I've seen legal assistants who jump from scheduling, to drafting a motion, to discovery responses, back to scheduling, all within the same hour, and do not really plan their work. This system may work and certainly everyone has their own style, however, it is usually not the most proficient way to toil away the workday in a business as high pressure as law can be. And, as a result, most of these legal assistants appear unorganized and are not shining examples of efficiency or productivity.

In addition to categorizing my work into specific types, such as scheduling, I also devised a general plan for what time of day I would do certain tasks. I know I am a morning person, a classic get-up-and-go type, and always have been. On a typical day, I would schedule in the morning mainly to get what was tedious and dreaded out of the way, when I had the most energy and motivation. Then, in the afternoon, I would work on projects (those tasks taking up a lot of time) such as discovery and miscellaneous matters such as catching up on correspondence. Of course, not every day can be dealt with this way, as other unforeseen tasks crop up or perhaps your attorney has a different set of things he or she wants to get done that day, but as a general rule, try to stick to your own, personalized schedule.

After a few months at the personal injury firm, and with my systems in place, I knew the cases, had a good flow of my work, and was generally very happy there.

To be thrown into a thicket of hard, mental labor and forced to really prove yourself is one of the best ways to learn and become self-sufficient and confident, I believe, even though it is also the scariest. Sometimes, when you are left with huge responsibility and minimal supervision, your desk may seem like an island, in the middle of an ocean of work with no escape or rescue in sight. But at those points, life survival skills take over and force you to just dive right into that sea of work, get it done, learn from trial and error, and move on to the next case. Somehow, you should always get to the surface, but with more experience and self-reliance for the next wave.

It seemed like this job finally fit into my life, and felt right with my ambitious personality.

## *PERSONALITY AND INTEREST VS. CAREER CHOICES*

I have long thought about the personality/interest vs. career phenomena. My own experiences taught me that, to be happiest at your workplace, one must achieve the right "fit". For some legal assistants, this means finding the area of law and the right environment that best suits your personality and/or your interests. I have actually conducted extensive research about this very issue for an article I was writing for the *National Paralegal Reporter.*

I found that legal assistants who seek out an area of law that best suits either their interests or their personality are far happier and content in their careers and their lives as a whole. But many never even think about this pairing of their true selves and their work.

How do you know or find out what type of individual you are? Think about your own personality for a moment. The term "personality" rose from "persona," which is Greek for the word "mask." Ancient Greek theatre actors wore masks to identify the different roles or personalities they were portraying in their plays. Think about your own "masks," which would include all of your attitudes, aptitudes, abilities, aspirations, habits, likes, dislikes, interests, special traits, wishes and goals. This will lead you to and identify your personality type. The way you act and react to your environment also helps to make up your personality. Hot tempers are normally labeled as "A" type and cool heads are more typically known as "B."

Much of what we know as personality type can really be classified or placed into what we already know has been defined as Type A and Type B personalities. Type A people are recognized as most always in a rush, being extremely industrious, ambitious and persistent. Type B persons are known for their easy-going demeanors and for being detail-oriented. Most people know from an early age what type they are, or to which type they more noticeably lean. Think back to your own childhood. Were you always content with puttering around with one thing at a time, with not a lot of structure? This points to a probable Type B. Or, were you happiest when you were highly scheduled with your school, soccer, karate, and pottery classes? If so, Type A seems more your mode. Either type has traits that lend themselves to the field of legal assisting and no matter what your personal pace, you can almost certainly find a perfect match in this arena.

For example, someone like myself, an admittedly uptight Type A, is better suited for a fast-paced litigation trial practice. An area such as probate or real estate would probably bore and frustrate me, especially given my tenure and experience with the insurance defense firm I described earlier.

Likewise, if you are a middle of the road Type B, somewhat of a bit less frenzied person, you would be more likely to fit best in a family law, bankruptcy or corporate atmosphere. Too much flurry and high-paced volume may leave you feeling frazzled. If, however, you enjoy working on detail oriented, methodical tasks, probate, real estate, or immigration law might be positive directions to seek for a proper pairing with your personality type. Type Bs are able to feel and enjoy a sense of accomplishment and validation even without the constant, urgent pressure of a trial practice.

You may also wish to blend an area of law with one or more of your interests. Perhaps you like music and sports. An entertainment, intellectual property, or sports law firm may be the key to marrying your true passions with your paralegal career. I once knew a paralegal who loved and participated avidly in extreme sports. He hit the slopes to snowboard on weekends and devoured anything to do with skateboarding. He found work at a firm specializing in representing ski resorts in various cases, including injuries occurring on ski slopes, chair lifts, the resort premises, zoning for runs, and the like. This particular job even afforded him the opportunity to be involved in parts of the acquisition and design of ski slopes and which areas would be designated for snowboarding. He absolutely loved his job and had truly found his own secret of success.

Likewise, if you love medicine, health care issues, and case studies of illnesses, injuries and maladies, you may be well suited for a personal injury or medical malpractice firm. Sifting through medical records, and properly organizing and summarizing notes and reports, is a huge part of this type of work.

If the craving of protecting natural resources is meaningful to you, a stint at a nature, environmental or maritime firm may be your ticket to making a difference. A friend of mine worked for an environmental firm for a while, assisting in situations which ran the gamut from enforcement of various park rules to illegal waste dumping within wildlife sanctuaries. She had literally found her "natural" calling.

Maybe helping elderly people is your mission. Working for an elder law, probate and estate planning firm will likely be your answer to "mission accomplished." My husband's friend from law school, along with his staff, finds great satisfaction in assisting his elderly clients through the estate planning process. We can all think about the eldest members of our family, and even ourselves, planning to go into a nursing home and the comfort of having an honest, helpful attorney and staff to assist in making the financial and emotional process easier and smoother.

Another compartment of the right fit in your career would be to think about what "side" you want to be on. For instance, do you like fighting for the rights of prisoners? Or do you prefer seeing that prisoners see their fair share of jail time and pay the price for their crimes? This could mean the difference in working for the office of the State Attorney or the Public Defender or criminal defense firm.

Are you passionate about working with your attorney to fight for the rights of consumers and the general public? Plaintiff's personal injury and products liability may be for you. Or, do you prefer to work with corporations to stop some of the seemingly meritless lawsuits that arise? If so, seek out defense firms who provide a defense for insurance companies and other corporations.

 **STOP! LEGAL TERMINOLOGY AHEAD!**

Okay, we've used the following terms before, but haven't properly defined them. So here goes:

Plaintiff: The party who institutes or commences a lawsuit or action is called the Plaintiff or the Petitioner. In civil lawsuits, Plaintiff is usually used, while in family law, depending on jurisdiction, Petitioner is more common. In criminal cases, the State or Commonwealth is the Plaintiff, with the accused being the Defendant.

Which necessarily brings us to:

Defendant: The party or parties against whom a lawsuit is filed. Also can be referred to as the Respondent.

There are also opportunities to be found in the military and in the field of teaching and education. Consult your career center, or spend some time researching on the Internet if these are avenues you might wish to take.

There are a virtually endless list of many other hobbies, dreams and passions to fuse with areas of law and types of law firms. No matter what your interest, pace or personality, there is almost certainly a place for you to unify your individual traits into your paralegal career. Finding the perfect mix is one of the keys to success in your career, and your life.

## *FINDING MY OWN NICHE*

My position at the fast-paced personal injury firm lasted five years. Though I predominantly handled personal injury and medical malpractice cases, I also learned criminal, family law, some limited probate, and bankruptcy law. We usually had a pretty well-rounded staff, although some of the staff turned over every now and then. And, we went from periods of being understaffed to sufficient staff. This was due to a variety of events such as changes in personnel, marketing, case loads, availability of qualified employees, and the quantity of work required for current cases.

The firm typically employed a receptionist, a few paralegals, a bookkeeper, case managers or claims administrators who essentially had the experience and authority to settle cases, and attorneys. At times, I worked with three or four attorneys; other times I only worked directly with my boss, the owner of the firm. And, as I indicated before, like in every office, here there were some very good, experienced, conscientious employees and also some very substandard individuals who simply did not do their work or slacked off. You could usually tell right away the standouts from the unmanageable. I preferred to regularly interact with the proficient, accomplished employees—persons from whom I could learn and whose work ethic I could respect. I made some valuable and lasting friendships through my work at this firm, which later helped me with networking and future career options.

As an interesting tangent, it is a good idea, and I always made it a practice, to keep an updated resume on hand, as you never know what can happen, and what opportunities may present themselves. Law firms go out of business, downsizing occurs, and yes, you can get fired unexpectedly, even if not justifiably. Working for lawyers will teach you that they can be a fickle sort. Or, you may also wish to quit to seize an opportunity of a lifetime that you just heard about. All of these are reasons to be prepared for any eventuality that might arise.

For the first time, I understood how important contacts and acquaintances could be. The adage of never burning a bridge holds true. The legal community, at least in a good percentage of areas, is quite small and surprisingly tight-knit, even in a large metropolitan area. Everyone seems to knows everyone, and gossip and occurrences spread through the ranks like wildfire. Bad reputations grow quickly and fester. Though no one can stay out of every string of gossip, I advise to try not to really bash anyone. I found the best thing to do is be a good listener and a good observer. And know whom to trust. Know in whom to confide and be careful even with these individuals as to how you characterize things. Remain professional where you can. If you ever find yourself the subject of gossip—whew!—good luck. It will be a tough haul, especially if the talk is scandalous. But really, if the gossip is not true, the best thing to do is hold your head up high, laugh it off, even joke about it and then, ignore it forever more. People will forget. If the gossip is true, well, fess up, admit your mistake and move on. Once the "behind the back" talk loses its luster, people will move on too, to their next "target."

My friends, contacts and colleagues would play an integral role in helping me through the next phase of my career.

By this point in time, I had worked two, sometimes three jobs to put my husband, Kevin, through law school. My contacts around town had gotten me typing jobs on the side of my regular employment, transcribing dictation tapes, research projects and various freelancing opportunities. I took nearly everything offered to me. As my husband could not work during law school, we needed the money. While still in the honeymoon phase of our infant marriage, my regular job at the personal injury firm and my side work permitted us to eke out our living through this money-crunching period. Kevin was able to work during the summers at law firms to gain experience and contribute extra income towards the ever-mounting bills. My husband sailed through the three years of law school, finally graduating. Did I say sail? Most of the time, for me, it was more like a slow drift on a leaking, rickety wooden raft, with land a long, long way off.

Yes, this time in our lives was tough, sometimes we were left wondering if we would actually make it. I oftentimes felt on the verge of sinking, but always remained afloat. But when it was finally over and he graduated, we chalked up the experience as one of the greatest character-building missions of our lives to date. We threw a huge party to celebrate the end of this trek. But another expedition was about to begin.

It was time for the universally dreaded Bar Exam.

**STOP! LEGAL TERMINOLOGY AHEAD!**

Bar Examination (and what is a "Bar" anyway?): Each state lays out the individual requirements for attorneys to practice law in that state. Each state's governing body for all attorneys licensed to practice law in that state is known as a "Bar Association," a nod to our country's heritage from British colonial times, where attorneys were known as "barristers" because they were the ones, along with Judges, Bailiffs, and parties, who were allowed to "cross the bar" separating the gallery from the actual litigants. In order to complete a license to practice law, prospective attorneys are tested in a grueling, two or three-day comprehensive test that usually includes several hundred multiple choice questions along with numerous essay questions and documents and cases to review and analyze. This test is known as the bar examination, and must be passed in order for an attorney to be admitted past the "bar."

I was barely allowed to speak with Kevin for the seven weeks prior to him sitting for the Bar—not that I wanted to, with as completely absorbed in his studies as he was! I was quite literally "barred" from him! He took a popular preparatory course for four of the seven weeks, early in the mornings, and then would hole up inside our home library for the rest of the day, every day, studying fervently until around midnight each night. He was taking practice exams almost daily and going over his books and notes from every class he took in law school. Keep in mind, this is a life-defining event for any person contemplating being an attorney—taking everything that you have learned in three years and being able to accurately apply it to very tricky questioning in a one-time test. And, failure meant the worst—one cannot practice law without successfully passing this examination. It was an extremely intense experience and the pressure was mounting for him as the bar examination loomed closer and closer.

On the other hand, I was excited because at this point, I was experiencing a bit of burnout in my career. Here I was, almost five years into my very solid job at the personal injury firm. I had great experiences under my belt, had attended trials with the attorney, and had a grip on the small details as well as the big picture of the legal system. At this point in my workplace, the staff had eroded somewhat.

Even though this had happened before, it seemed that the lackadaisical people I worked with aggravated me more and more and I couldn't quite understand why they did not get written up, dealt with or fired. I also tired of the seemingly shoddy work ethic shrouding my office and the societal opinion of personal injury lawyers as "ambulance chasers." The blaring, outrageous lawsuit headlines such as the various class action tobacco cases, suing fast food companies for making people fat, the infamous hot coffee in the lap, all helped to, in my opinion, create, instill, and foster a sense of entitlement in the general public, including some of our clients. In other words, I was losing touch with the personal nature of the meaning and purpose of my work. There seemed to be little personal responsibility, ethics, morals or standards that I could unearth, and it was affecting me as a result. But evidence of the public's sense of entitlement to filing lawsuits over every little thing, and the relative level of absurdity of these cases, was growing with each day I continued in this firm. Couldn't people just talk things out anymore? Didn't people have any problem-solving skills whatsoever? Whatever happened to hashing things out over a cup of coffee (not too hot, of course)? It used to be that suing someone was a last resort after attempts to settle a claimed grievance failed, almost prohibitively expensive and protracted, and occurred only in egregious situations. Now, if you so much as look at someone out of the corner of your eye, you're sued!

This is what I meant when I said that in this profession you will see societal problems and broad commentary on the legal field in general and try to work with and find solutions to them. Of course, the lawyers, doctors and political leaders around the country saw this emerging trend as well, and proposed one tort reform or damage capping solution after another. To date, for all their hard work in identifying the problems, and trying to find solutions, I personally believe the biggest change will occur when there is education of the people (perhaps starting in early school years?) to include problem-solving skills (communication proficiency), coping skills (something bad happened to you? Well, that's just *life*. Find a way to overcome it and move on), diminishing a sense of entitlement (thinking one is entitled to money just for getting a bad rap), and the all-important skill of personal responsibility (maybe it isn't anyone's fault but your own that you slipped and fell), along with some reform of the insurance industry and the monopolistic stranglehold it seems to have on the purse-strings in this country. Of course, not every individual acts or feels this way, and of course, there are truly negligent occurrences happening today for which one *should* seek compensation; it's just that a generally litigious mind set seems to have taken a hold on society, as a mass, and seems to have infiltrated how we go about our lives. I mean, every television network prominently features programs glamorizing the lives of beautiful, zealously advocating attorneys, championing some cause or another. Movies are no different, also (fictionally, mind you) creating a portrait that attorneys and the law should be a first resort rather than a last. Change must begin with each person.

During this spell of searching for principles and reason in my career, I witnessed the disastrous campaigns some employees got away with and the resultant havoc such behavior can generate upon the morale of an office. Around this time, my boss's daughter came to work for the firm, straight out of law school. She had never worked before and was, quite bluntly, a spoiled brat. She proceeded to try to run all over the rest of us employees. I, being raised to not accept people who demean others, was appalled and I felt trapped by a situation I could not control. I will give you an example.

One particular day, the phones were overly busy. They simply would not stop ringing and the receptionist could not get to some calls due to being already on three or four other lines. All of the rest of the staff, me included, attempted to answer the overflow calls, but this day was busier than most, and each of us were inhibited by several other tasks and meetings which came up on this maniacal day. Most of us were already on other calls and we simply could not get to every phone call that went unanswered. These calls were set up to transfer automatically to voice mail in this type of situation, and we would retrieve messages immediately each day. All of us were professionals and realized the importance of answering a phone in an office, but this day was atypically inundated—some days are just like that.

But the daughter, nicknamed "The Tyrant" by the office employees for just such behavior as I will describe, stomped out of her office and yelled at the top of her lungs "The phone is ringing, PEOPLE!"

Well then.

I recall thinking, "I guess we were <u>her</u> 'people' now and, apparently, we were deaf to boot!"

We *heard* the phones, we just couldn't do everything all the time! She had treated the staff like that since her first day in the office—as inferiors to be looked down upon and yelled at. You will find all types in law firms, and some attorneys are more difficult than others, and have a reputation, often well-deserved, for such behavior. I for one was fatigued in continually dealing with a person whose modus operandi was to belittle the staff at every turn she had, and was frankly sick of such treatment. This would turn out to be one of the main factors contributing to my eventually leaving the firm.

The Tyrant's daily mean-spirited behavior took a toll on the staff as well. We were walking on eggshells and cringed when we saw her, because we never knew what exhortation would spew forth from her biting mouth at any given time. The general opinion around the office was that none of us liked her. It was as if she did not have a clue as to her tyranny, or the power of self-realization. I think her actions gave her a false sense of power and prestige, but it simply darkened her to the rest of us and made her look, well, foolish, in our eyes. If she couldn't even control her own behavior, how could she issue spot properly, practice law ethically, and help others?

My boss, her father, seemed oblivious to his daughter's abrasive personality, or chose to ignore it. Once, though, after yet another diabolical outburst, he quickly ran into her office and shut the door. It was our hope that he was finally seeing the effect of her behavior and, with his vast experience in handling varying sorts of people and employees, was trying to teach her how to conduct herself in a professional environment. But generally, people don't change and unfortunately this was the case here—no amount of counseling or teaching could make this attorney even close to a hands-on "people person," and her behavior grew more outrageous and damaging to the employees.

The field of law is, at times, a very stressful way to make a living, with the work load, the relative high stakes and the differing personalities. This seems to bring out some people's unscrupulous character traits and magnify them a hundred-fold. A certain portion of the people who choose a legal career path in the first place are those who are confident, assertive and egoists to some degree. Some might call them rude, arrogant and full of themselves! But they are out there and this is where people skills, patience, and your own confidence will come into play.

What exactly happened in my situation?

From then on, since the tension in the office was mounting, my solution was to walk into the office every day, sit down and work. I avoided The Tyrant at all costs and every necessary contact would be in writing, or followed up with a memo. This was my protection, my fortress, with which I surrounded myself for my own protection. Luckily, my boss (her father) and I always maintained a great working relationship. He always "saw through" office politics and luckily, after working together closely for nearly five years, he knew me as a person well enough to respect me as well as my work. I will always remember him fondly.

My stronghold philosophy worked until I eventually left the firm. Yes, sometimes problems simply won't go away and you have to deal with them in any way you can, in as healthy a manner as you can. Ignoring the problem and keeping your distance is, sometimes, a better solution if not the *only* solution. In most offices, there is usually someone who doesn't get along with others, and usually there is at least one you will not get along with, for whatever reason.

On the other hand, while we are on the subject, sometimes it takes an already out of control situation, and massive staff turnover to result in a pervasive office problem finally being dealt with. I have also seen very competent, excellent people work for decades in firms, only to be fired over some silly mistake or dispute or even downsizing and layoffs.

The lesson learned for either scenario? Have a good work ethic, try to get along with everyone, but look to yourself first for solutions to problems and keep yourself informed, and content. Just as in any profession, and life in general, know your friends and your enemies and watch out for number one— yourself. There are many good people you will meet—people from whom you can learn and respect and who will enrich your life. I have met many people like this and I have tried to emulate their habits. And if you are the one persons look up to and ask advice from, what a wonderful feeling to be a mentor and to be revered in that way. You, making a difference to others, can be a fantastically rewarding aspect of your life.

I would, after a long, frustrating time, learn that to solve a problem such as this, *I* would be the one who had to change, or alter how I dealt with such situations. I learned to simply not think about such conduct, shrug it off and not obsess over it, as I had always done. In the past, I would constantly wonder why someone felt compelled to act in such a way, and what I could do to change it. I had to agonize and learn for myself over many years that I would never figure out *all* of the circumstances going on in someone's mind enough to decode and deal with their more negative personality traits. More importantly, even if I could figure a person out, I could certainly do nothing to change someone who did not want to change themselves. Beating myself up for a solution to an unsolvable problem adds nothing to an equation except for self-imposed, damaging stress and heartache. As much as I hate to advocate anything less than complete and utter organization and perfection in the workplace, in a limited number of situations, indifference can be the key to dealing effectively— to not either *actively* hate or loathe, but to accept the situation as it is and that it cannot be changed. I have only more recently learned to not obsess over every negative aspect regarding lawyers and the practice of law.

While I was learning more of my life's lessons, in the meantime, my husband remained studying in the library until the day of the Bar exam.

The day loomed bright and clear, but oppressively hot and humid, an obvious harbinger of the brutal test my husband had to master. The short drive to the city's convention center, where the bar examination was being held for the entire state, was too short, I'm sure, for him. His, and my, whole future rested on his passing this arduous and punishing two-day examination, this life-defining event.

The two days passed. We glanced at each other in the evenings; ate dinner in virtual silence. I saw stress percolating in his every cell. I was practically boiling with anxiety also, but didn't let on. I tried not to talk him too much, because I could see that he had a single-minded purpose in the test, and I did not want to turn him from that focus.

Finally, day two ended. Then, the long wait for the results. He could not honestly estimate how he had done on the exam when he finished. I don't think anyone can! He felt as everyone who had taken it felt—that it was one of the more difficult things they had ever done, and it was truly a test, of more than just knowledge—also of quick thinking and dealing with adversity.

"Results day," the day when the results of the Bar are posted online, finally came. Physically shaking, he scrolled down the internet page and looked for his name. He had passed all three sections, the State, the Multi-State, and the essay portion!

I think our entire family was on the phone with each other in the space of seconds! We were all so happy for him, for us, and I was ecstatic! I could finally see a glimpse of the proverbial light at the end of the tunnel and perhaps, a start to my long sought after writing career.

But after the relieved and excited celebration, we realized he still didn't really have employment, or a concrete offer in which he was interested. Several positions for which he had interviewed had been offered, but he had not formally accepted anything, and moreover, he was not sure that he was interested in climbing the corporate ladder of the medium and large sized law firms. In truth, he seemed to be hearing the same mantra from the attorneys who were conducting the interviews—that he would be expected to bill at least two thousand to twenty-five hundred hours per year for the firm, which equated to approximately a minimum fifty to sixty hour work week, that he would be the, "low man on the totem pole," and thus expected to cover less interesting hearings and depositions, and that he would be assigned to whichever attorney and area of law with which the firm decided to place him.

Kevin has a huge independent streak in him, and cannot reconcile conformity or the traditional norms of living the "rat race," so to speak. In short, he is a free thinker, motivated by his own pace, likes to make his own decisions, and often takes the unconventional and not easy road. Therefore, he and I were contemplating other, bigger, things.

An attorney I knew and had worked with at the afore-mentioned personal injury firm had left to go out on his own and, "hang out his shingle." He rented space close to where we lived, and had an extra office available. My husband and I slowly formulated and implemented the idea that he would rent space there and open up his own law practice. We sketched out a business plan, with start-up costs, hourly rates, billing procedures, and marketing criteria.

Were we crazy? Yes! Completely!

But we did not yet have children. We also did not have a house or mortgage, and he desperately yearned to practice music and entertainment law, an area of law that really could not be found in our area. Music is my husband's absolute

passion, as writing is mine. When he was a member of a budding band in his earlier years, he had been presented with recording contracts, tour contracts, royalty
statements, etc. He remembered a time when he sought explanations and assistance with all the contractual jargon and could not find the answers locally, and
therefore did not have the benefit of adequate or competent counsel in his musi-
cal endeavors, and likely waived one or more of his rights. There were simply very
few attorneys practicing music and entertainment law at that time in this area.
Kevin remembered this, recognized the need for a practitioner in this area, and
wanted to fill that need.

We conducted some market research, spoke with friends of my husband in
local bands, and found that there was a living to be made in this area of law as it
was long-neglected. My husband even had plenty of contacts from when he
drummed, "back in the day." And, I was interested in finding out more about a
field that represented musicians, as well as authors, screenplay writers and the
like. Here, I was also combining my interests into an area of law.

We decided to go for it.

Kevin allotted himself three weeks to get all of the many tasks necessary to
open a business, such as business and occupational licensing, liability insurance, a
desk, chairs, computers, a copier, fax machine, supplies, purchasing phone lines
and numbers, as well as other duties, done. He actually beat his deadline by four
days. I told you he is motivated. In just over two weeks' time, we had rented the
available office, and suddenly, we had a working law office!

About three months after opening the firm, I also quit my job at the personal
injury firm and went to work for the attorney who agreed to share space with
Kevin, so that I could be close to him and help him build his practice. Kevin and
he would share my legal assisting services and skills, which would let me keep a
close eye on the particulars of our business. The attorney was a friend of mine
who I always got along with, worked very well with, and liked. This was a bless-
ing to me because I had been unhappy at my job, largely due to The Tyrant and
the tense atmosphere that ensued and I was ready for a change. Also, I could be
close to my husband and help him begin and run his law practice. I had tons of
ideas on the best ways to set things up from its inception, organizationally, to
build the business, and had lots of hope and ambition.

I had regained my fire about the practice of law and my role therein.

When I gave my two weeks' notice to my boss, he was noticeably disappointed
and disheartened that I was leaving, but realized that I was making an important
decision in my life, and for the career of both me and my husband. He told me I
was the best legal assistant he had ever had in twenty-five years of practice, a wonderful compliment from a man with such worldly experience. I left satisfied;
knowing I had done a good job for him. And I kept my mouth shut about The

Tyrant. Those things will always come out in the wash, as my mother says. I don't even speak of her in this book for bashing reasons. Rather, I relate my experience because people skills are so crucial and there is usually at least *someone* you cannot get along with in the workplace no matter how hard you try and one must learn to deal with this fact. I also want to emphasize that not every problem is going to go away—sometimes changing yourself and/or your situation is the best route.

Most greatly admired business leaders relay that if someone is an absolute genius at his or her job, but can't get along with people, they are useless. I agree wholeheartedly. Think about this. If another legal assistant is horrible to you every day and suddenly asks you for a favor while in the middle of a rush job, are you really going to jump when she asks you to? No! In fact, just the opposite. You may likely say you can't help, or don't know the answer to her question, even if you do. People want to help other people who are nice and who respect everyone else. Period.

I suppose I could have asked my boss for a sit-down and tried to talk the problems out with him and his daughter, but I honestly don't think it would have helped, at least not permanently. Disputes relating to actual work may be dealt with this way. Personality conflicts are much harder as, essentially, you are asking someone to change their very being. This, unfortunately, is difficult to do even if one is motivated properly. If one does not see a reason for change, it customarily will simply not happen.

My new position working in the same office as my husband was exciting. We drove into work together and ate lunch together. Luckily, we are one of those couples who like spending a lot of our time together and can get along well at work and at home. And, technically, I worked full-time for the other attorney anyway, so I did not work with my husband *per se* during the day, although my desk was about eight feet from his office door. I answered his phones and did some minor scheduling, but by and large, I had my own job to think about, and he his.

What I did to assist Kevin and our business was to arrive about an hour early in the mornings to help him with his work, work some nights after 5:00 p.m., and work on weekends where we had to. At that time, we lived only about 5 minutes from our office and I would pop in on Saturday or Sunday mornings for a few hours and help him prepare correspondence, pleadings and do some filing. Also, keep in mind that my husband opened a business essentially straight out of law school—and they don't teach you how to either run a business or to practice law in law school, only to think like an attorney. So, if we were to succeed, it would take both of us contributing, and my experience would be crucial in defining Kevin's own untested work ethic, and help to fill in the gaps.

At this new job, I felt more at ease and less stressed at first as I worked for only one attorney, the one who shared space with my husband—not two, three or more, as had been the case at the personal injury law firm. There were only about sixty open cases total and it was practically all personal injury litigation—something I knew very well at this point.

I settled into my new job with a fresh, renewed enthusiasm and started the same way as with my previous jobs. I created a master list of all cases, and organized the work. The secretary prior to me was a mess, with seemingly few usable organizational procedures, aside from eight or nine "piles" scattered in various places about the office that I suppose had significance only to her. It took me a week to get a grip on pending work and things that had to be addressed, just to make sure that no deadlines were being missed. But, in my usual fashion, I planned, organized, obtained trays, and put my "system" in place.

After a few months at this new position, with the added responsibility of assisting Kevin with his business, which I thought would be so much better, I became the most stressed and unenthusiastic in my life. I became overwhelmed with two law firms, two case loads, and I would see if I had what it took to overcome further adversity and uncertainty, all the while fretting about my husband's fledgling and still precarious young business.

At this point, Kevin and I had a plan. I would continue to work full time, and then, when the business got up and running, finance and productivity wise, I would simply work with him exclusively. I thought it would be within the year.

In actuality, it would be more than four years by the time I could even seriously think about this situation becoming a reality.

## *BUILDING A BUSINESS*

Patience. That is what I lacked. I simply had too unrealistic an expectation. I really thought that I could work with my husband and our law firm would be self-sustaining in no time. By this time, a little over a year into opening his practice, we had bought our first home. Even though the home was certainly within our means, I had to keep working. I desperately wanted to work with my husband and experience the seeming freedoms he seemed to be enjoying by working for himself. I wanted to take off on a Wednesday afternoon if I wanted to! Or kick-off the weekend at 2:00 p.m. on Friday. Not like he did this too often, as he was struggling just to keep up with the workload, as it was only himself, and me when I could help. But he *could* take such liberties if he wished, and that is a large attraction to running one's own business. I also yearned for more time to devote to my writing.

I never really contemplated becoming a freelance legal assistant, but now I understood how much of an urge it could be to work for one's self. Though it was my husband's law firm, I felt an integral part of it by setting it up, creating procedures, organizing the forms, implementing filing systems, and studying different marketing methods. I also worked there on my "off time" and felt I was working towards financial and personal freedom for both of us.

To those contemplating a freelance or independent business, it will probably be the hardest you will work in your life. But oh how rewarding it can be if you stay focused and follow your plan! If you have persistence, perseverance and perspiration, you have a great chance of making it! But if this is a road you should choose to travel, be prepared.

You will likely worry about making the bills every month, even when the money is flowing well. There are ups and down, peaks and valleys, good months and bad months. As a sole practitioner attorney friend of my husband once told him, "a sole practitioner is neither rich for long nor poor for long." The best thing we did was actually follow the advice of my father and stash three months worth of expenses in our firm operating account (some money managers suggest six, or even nine months). We had this sum in our account at all times in case there was a slow month or in case of unexpected financial circumstances. If we ever dipped into it, during a bad cycle for instance, we would first and foremost, replenish it and go from there. This was difficult to do, as it is very tempting to take that money and spend it, but the peace of mind was worth every penny saved.

It all sounded so easy. I thought, well, Kevin will bill $150.00 per hour, times $X$ hours to get the amount we needed and wanted. With that formula, we should be able to make an outstanding living. What I didn't take into account was clients not paying their bills, on time or at all. Billing is easy, and there are several software programs available to make it easier to bill for legal services. Actually *collecting* on all of the accounts receivable once invoiced and sent out remains one of small businesses' most frustrating tasks.

Whatever money we made every month would go to pay the bills, and whatever was left over, but never dipping into our three month uncertainty stockpile, we took as a salary. This is a good system, one that can be used quite successfully for freelancers and sole practitioners. You can modify it to pay yourself twice a month or even weekly, just so long as the emergency supply is not affected but in the event of an actual financial crisis, such as the phones threatened to be turned off, or something similar.

In two years' time, the business was somewhere past fledgling and we had learned a lot about marketing and building a client base. We truly did it one client at a time. To get the word out, we signed on with a legal referral business where, for a set fee per month, the referral service would forward client calls to us. At the time, Kevin decided to take criminal clients, as it was an area of law, even though he was really not interested in from a "calling" standpoint, was a mostly up front and cash area of law, which he quickly mastered, and could do most of the work himself, since I was still his secretary/paralegal during my "off" hours.

I still remember the very first call from a potential client in jail—at 2:10 in the morning on a Thursday night! But Kevin spoke with the gentleman for a while, gathered his facts and achieved a very positive result when he was able to make a motion to the Court during business hours. This client then told a couple of other inmates and their friends, and after a few months, we had a criminal defense practice blooming. My husband toiled away to do the best job he could for his clients—he got cases dismissed, charges reduced, violations of probation set aside, and post judgment motions made and granted. The clients, in turn, referred their friends and family. Kevin argued some pretty dramatic motions in front of the circuit judges, and the shackled defendants would be clamoring for his business card. That is how we built our business.

At first, we practiced what is called "rent law" or taking whatever case walked through the door just to pay the rent. This was also a veritable "trial by fire," not only for Kevin, but for me to learn even more areas of law to help him as his *de facto* paralegal. I brushed up on family law, contracts and consumer law, criminal law, and probate law such as wills, living wills, and the like so that I could help him with forms, scheduling, correspondence, and the other daily tasks of a case. He also was working hard to establish a niche in the field he really yearned for success in—music and entertainment law. He held free quarterly seminars at local music stores about various topics in music law that were of importance to musicians and artists. He did this as a service to the community, but obviously this would and did have marketing aspects as well, and Kevin still has clients from those days, even though the music store has long since closed down.

He hooked up with a regional entertainment magazine to write a monthly column about music law and related topics, which again resulted in increased clientele. These articles could be quite involved in legal issues and clauses, and generally demonstrated to the public that Kevin knew what he was talking about. Creative marketing, as well as word of mouth helped build this portion of the practice.

This is where I affirmed anew what an asset a good legal assistant can be to an attorney, and how, in crunch times, a legal assistant who steps up to a challenge is invaluable. I know, I know, it *was* my husband, after all, didn't he already think I walk on water?

Together, we slowly realized what areas of law were more manageable than others, which were lucrative, and what made a difference to us at the end of the day. We also learned more practical things, such as proper choice, implementation, and use of a software filing and case management system, an office supply inventory, obtaining the best prices on long distance service and computers, and where to find cheap office furniture. We also tried a couple of ways to keep track of billable time before we settled on a system that would work and that he would actually use. Starting truly from scratch and constantly reviewing policies and procedures afforded us the opportunity of seeing immediately what did and did not work from a productivity standpoint.

But Kevin did not take to my personal "filter" system, mainly because he just didn't use it and never got into it, and had no background with it. He preferred an in-box and a couple of filing folders for managing his active work. He also preferred looking at the entire file instead of breaking the work down into so many little tasks like I favored.

So, a great legal assistant not only establishes a pleasant working camaraderie with his or her attorney, but respects others' own work habits and preferences. A good working team will exhibit a combination of the organizational skills of both the legal assistant and the attorney—each respecting the other and what each likes and dislikes, what works and what does not. Collaboration and teamwork is one the fundamental keys to success.

We also made sure not to put all our eggs in one basket; meaning, Kevin never just practiced music law, only criminal law, or exclusively family law. An amalgamation of several areas of law usually makes a firm, big or small, better equipped to handle downturns in economies, and general declines in business. For example, if family law intakes were down for a couple of months, the criminal cases usually were up. Some firms are "boutique" firms and only practice exclusive, niche-oriented law. These usually have superb reputations in the particular area of law, but they are also prone to bad economic times as they have nothing to fall back on if their one and only area of practicing takes a turn for the worse.

I also learned a lot more about the paralegal profession and what is takes to be well-rounded, flexible and resourceful. I believe relaying my personal experiences of helping to open, start and build a law firm will give readers a peek into possibly sparking their own paralegal business or to better prepare them if their attorney asks them, as their trusted and loyal paralegal, to go with them when they leave a big firm and start their own firm.

The years went by and the business settled into a nice flow. We've since endured moving Kevin's offices to bigger quarters, and my slowly easing into working exclusively with my husband. Our quality of life, both at home and at work, is nothing short of fantastic, thanks to the many years of staying four or five hours after close of regular business to ensure ourselves of success, and through staying the course in the face of sometimes daunting adversity.

And, like all cycles, the one I was feeling of being the Queen of Stress-dom and worrying about crushing amounts of work, would soon pass too, and I got back on track, feeling motivated and relaxed again.

How do I look back and remember these early years and look towards the future? It was a time of great obstacles, building, uncertainties, but greater rewards. The journey was sometimes demanding and off-course, tangential even, but we always eventually got back on track further up the road. And some of the views along the way were out of this world. Our souls felt worthwhile, gratified, satisfied.

I see an even brighter future ahead.

# CHAPTER III

# THE WORK

So now that you have a background of the legal assistant profession and my own personal experiences, what does "assist attorneys" really mean? What is the work actually like?

In a nutshell, it means you will do anything and everything your boss or supervisor tells you to do, and some they don't. It means doing a lot or most of the work that attorneys used to do exclusively. But, let's get beyond these phrases and probe into what the work is really like, the world of working for attorneys and what you will be doing every single day as a paralegal.

You will answer phones, speak and meet with clients, type letters and memos, draft and write pleadings, motions, and memoranda, run (sometimes literally) to the courthouse, research, do some investigative work and handle case management duties. If you are in a small office or work for a sole practitioner, you may be called upon to be a *de facto* receptionist, greeting clients, getting them coffee or a soft drink, making copies, billing for the attorney, paying his taxes, making sure his bar dues are up-to-date, and a myriad of other organizational tasks and beyond. And, in classic lawyer talk, your job is to make your attorney "look as good as possible," in as many facets of the practice as you are able.

Aside from practicing excellent ethics, about the only limitation on legal assistants is making absolutely sure to *not* give out legal advice, let the attorney set fees for legal services, and understand that the attorney is directly responsible for representing the clients—for the most part. Even representation of clients in court, usually confined to attorneys, has been allowed of paralegals in some very limited and controlled settings in certain jurisdictions, although it is not widespread at the moment. "Legal advice" is, sometimes, hard to define. One good rule to live by, is that if you find yourself saying something such as, "I advise…" or, "I think you should…" or something like that, stop! To avoid the problem and potential pitfall of possibly practicing law without a license, which is a criminal offense in most states, legal assistants cannot give legal advice, advise clients or anyone what to do legally, or render a legal opinion, even if they know the answer or know exactly what the client should do. Be careful when answering questions such as statute of limitations deadlines, what to allege in a complaint, or if you think a person has a case or not. After consulting your attorney, you can relay the information from the attorney to the client, such as, "The attorney, Mr. Smith, would like me to relay to you that he does not feel he could assist you in this matter; however, he urges you to seek other opinions." But, it's always good practice for the actual lawyer to talk to a client, potential or otherwise, directly about such matters. It is safer and won't even give the illusion of doling out legal advice.

Paralegals can state procedural steps to a client, and assist with filling out forms such as divorce forms, just as independent paralegals do with the public, but you cannot advise what is required, legally, to allege in the forms.

Throughout the research and ultimate writing of this book, I have consulted with several attorneys, and wish to emphasize that nothing in this book should be construed as legal advice for anyone, or any situation. A foolproof motto: if ever in doubt, consult an attorney.

From the very beginning of a case, to the end, you, as a paralegal will likely have your hand in most every aspect. For most areas of civil law, learning how to draft complaints or petitions is invaluable if you are on the plaintiff's or petitioner's side; knowing when and how to answer a complaint or petition is critical on the defense side.

Learning to spot "red flags," or "hot button" issues will also be part of your job. For example, matters to carefully watch for may include counterclaims, because they require action such as an answer, motions to dismiss, or direction to the client to turn to their insurance company to provide them with a defense. Red flags also include requests for admissions and other discovery requests, because if these requests made by the opposing side, asking your client to admit or deny certain allegations, are not answered within a certain time period usually set out by statute or by local or administrative order, they are usually deemed admitted, or any defenses thereto are deemed waived. Other concerns may include medical records from different doctors with conflicting opinions, vague contract language, and certain motions, such as summary judgment motions. Calendaring these matters before they become tardy and negatively affect a client's case is crucial.

**STOP! LEGAL TERMINOLOGY AHEAD!**

Summary Judgment or Motion for Summary Judgment: One of the most critical junctures in any case is when a summary judgment issue or motion arises or is filed. "Summary Judgment" refers to the doctrine that one side uses against the other in a lawsuit, that the other side has failed to state a cause of action for which relief can be granted, that, even if taken as true, there are no material facts in dispute, and therefore, as a matter of law, the court can dismiss the case, summarily granting judgment without necessity of a trial on the merits. These motions can be extremely involved, and are usually accompanied by stout memoranda, replete with case law, and deep legal argument either for or against the notion of summary judgment. Usually happens towards the middle of a case, but this is not a rule.

Most of the work you do will either be initiative, meaning you and your firm will initiate something such as discovery, or a motion; or responsive, such as a document received from the opposing side requiring a response or some other action on your part.

Try to learn, as fast and efficiently as possible, the procedural rules for your particular jurisdiction along with the deadlines attached to each task, and what responsive action is needed for each document you see. Your attorney, or another legal assistant, will be glad to point you in the right direction for the location of these rules. For example, if you see a motion for summary judgment cross your desk, you will know that this is a dispositive motion, or a motion that can dispose of the case. In layman's terms, you could win or lose based on this motion without ever going to trial on the merits of the case! In our jurisdiction, a response to a motion for summary judgment is due five days prior to the hearing on the motion (not the date of the filing of the motion, but the hearing date upon which the motion will be heard by the court) or two days prior to the hearing if by hand-delivery to the opposing counsel's office. I usually calendar at least twenty to thirty days prior to a hearing date to start obtaining controverting affidavits, if need be, prepare a response, or to remind the attorney to start researching (or if that's your job, you will start researching the issues).

Thinking ahead and building in plenty of time on your calendar for problems and deadlines will make your, and your attorney's life, much smoother and easier. Unforeseen events do occur, and can be as innocuous as a day with twenty more phone calls than usual or three clients stopping in unexpectedly, to an undertaking as disruptive as a new client coming in at 2:00 p.m. who desperately needs a lawsuit filed by 5:00 p.m. that day in order to beat a statute of limitation or repose.

As with most practices, discovery tools and tasks are likely how a huge chunk of your time will be spent completing. It is an area where paralegals are greatly utilized by attorneys and law firms. Discovery documents consist typically of interrogatories, which are a series of written questions propounded upon a party to answer relating to a particular case, and requests for production of documents, such as police reports, medical records, policies of insurance, and contracts. Requests for Admissions are another useful instrument, and, as stated earlier, are "red flags" that must be acted upon as soon as possible upon receipt, as they must be completed by the client and then reviewed by the attorney, so they may require advanced calendaring foresight. These are basically questions or statements that one party asks the other to admit or deny. But remember, in most jurisdictions, if these are not answered in a timely manner, all statements or questions are deemed admitted—a possibly catastrophic event that could cripple the client's cause.

Depositions are extremely useful ways of obtaining information. More than likely, your job will be to actually schedule depositions of clients, witnesses, and experts, choose and hire the reporting service that will transcribe the deposition, and prepare your attorney for the deposition by compiling all documents needed for that particular deposition and making sure filing is up to date in the particular file. You will need to make sure you have all documentation and research needed for use in the deposition, and following up to obtain any transcripts your attorney may request, and make sure they are filed with the court, if needed. I do not go with my attorney to depositions and do not personally know of any paralegals that do; however, I know that some paralegals, typically in medium to large firms, do go with their attorneys to take notes, and generally assist the attorney with whatever may be needed.

Production from non-parties to the lawsuit, including subpoenaing records and other materials, can occupy a substantial portion of the work in some cases. Lawyers often gather information from various non-parties, that is, everyone and everything besides the parties named in a lawsuit, in order to verify the authenticity of what the parties say, argue, or posit. These materials can be anything from surveillance tapes of a suspected shoplifter from a grocery store, to medical records from a hospital, to telephone call logs or records. Each jurisdiction differs in the procedural rules for obtaining non-party production, such as what can be subpoenaed, how to subpoena, who issues a subpoena, or other measures that may be used in lieu of subpoenaing. Since a good portion of a paralegal's efforts goes towards obtaining, keeping track of, and assisting an attorney in utilizing these various non-party records, grasp the rules in your particular geographical area without delay. As stated earlier, your attorney, or another legal assistant, will be glad to point you in the right direction for the location of these rules. If you do not have these resources, try calling the Clerk of Court in your jurisdiction to inquire about obtaining a copy of the Local Rules, which are rules governing procedure in a particular jurisdiction.

When preparing or responding to discovery, learn how to look through the entire file for any little notes or facts that merit special attention. Educate yourself on your firm's particular system of attorney notes, intake notes, and other such banter between attorney and client. These are where you may find tidbits of treasured information that can help you take charge of a case or caseload and maximize your productivity and worth to your attorney.

It is also a good idea to meet, face to face, with a client, to go over each and every interrogatory question, or request for documents or admissions. This way, you cover everything all at once, and you can listen to their responses and ask for elaboration on anything you feel needs a bit more explaining or expanding. In the worst case scenario, a bit of issue-spotting on your part, and dutiful reporting back to the attorney on the client's relative strengths or weaknesses may save a potentially fatal or damaging gaff by the client down the road, especially one that might result in a time crunch or a discovery deadline issue.

Amendments and supplements will be some of your best friends, as they are sometimes used to correct mistakes. Most of the time, amendments and supplements are used to clarify, change or add to a document. But, if you, under the supervision of an attorney, make a mistake (and everyone makes mistakes!), and file something with, say the wrong caption, you can, depending on the situation and procedures for a particular jurisdiction, file anything from a simple amendment of that document with the corrections, to drafting a motion to correct what is commonly called scrivener's error, which is excusable error or neglect by a clerical assistant, not the attorney. If you send out a notice of taking deposition and send it out with the wrong date and time, you can usually simply file an amended notice of taking deposition with the corrected date and time. If you forget to list a witness on a witness list, you may be able to file a supplemental witness list to add the forgotten soul. Again, learn the rules and regulations in your jurisdiction.

Preparing motions is a pretty large portion of my work also, and I always start out with the question, "what am I asking the court to do?" A motion is simply asking the court to initiate some action or to *undo* some action—you are "moving" the court to act, as courts, except in rare circumstances, do not act on their own. It is asking the court (the judge) for what you want. Of course, proper groundwork must be laid before you will get what you want. For a motion to compel discovery, you should not just state, "The defendant was supposed to mail his response to request for production and he hasn't done so." You should state the background, and go through the situation chronologically, methodically, and logically, such as:

> Plaintiff propounded her Request for Production on June 9, 2002. *(Always state the exact name of the document, such as Request for Production, for uniformity and clarity)*
>
> The Defendant's response was due on July 9, 2002.
> As of the date of the filing of this motion, no response has been received.
>
> Plaintiff has made a good faith effort to obtain said responses and has been unable to do so.
>
> *(Most jurisdictions define "Good faith efforts" as contacting the opposing counsel or writing a letter to the opposing counsel requesting the status of the request and to give them a "heads up" that they are overdue and will face a motion to compel, or similar action.)*
>
> WHEREFORE, Plaintiff requests this Honorable Court to compel Defendant to deliver said response to Plaintiff's Request for Production, within ten (10) days of an order entered hereon.
>
> *(This language, of course, can be altered to match your jurisdictional requirements, and your lawyer's personal style, but always remember to summarize what you are asking the court to do, and it is a good idea to be very specific and lay out deadlines and time limits clearly)*

Writing clearly, logically and with brevity takes practice and skill. Writing, which is arguably the greatest invention and communication tool created by mankind, will be behind most things you do, be it a letter to a client, a demand letter to an opposing party, a motion or order, a memorandum of law, a memo to a file, a simple phone message, or a note to your boss.

Writing, from the oldest known form arising around 3000 B.C. until modern times, with over 6,000 languages, from logos, symbols, alphabets, and hieroglyphics, from alpha to omega, has predestined power and progress in a society. Writing and the spread of information, in a permanent form, is supremacy, and learning to use it is the crucial step up to the top of the pedestal. It is also absolutely integral to the practice of law, as most motions, and verily, all lawsuits, must be drafted and written up before they can be filed with the court.

Some view legal writing as dry and unimaginative, but it doesn't have to be! You can get creative, as long as you state your purpose plainly.

When I used to write demand letters, which are letters outlining facts, theories of liability, and demanding settlement to an opposing party or its representative such as an insurance adjuster, I used to use some creative spark to infuse plot, suspense, and characters into the letter. Of course, I never just made things up or used overly exaggerated facts. I simply used these elements of literature to liven things up. But a good bit of inflammatory language and creative hyperbole goes a long way in making a demand seem much more involving than dreary.

For example, your assignment is to write a demand letter for your client, a person injured in a motor vehicle accident. Your firm probably has forms you can use as a template to get started. You could just plug the information in and be done with it. But why not have a little fun? Let's see how.

Who are the characters? The people involved in the car accident. Players may also include the investigating officer who wrote up an accident report, witnesses, and passengers.

What is the plot? The physical vector of the automobile accident and its aftermath on the people involved, is the central conflict in the "story."

Then, you can delve into more of the basics of journalism and reporting.

Where did the accident happen?

When did it happen?

Why did it happen?

How did it happen?

Also, think about the theme of your character or story.

I once wrote up a summary of a client who was a young mother. She had injured her back in an accident and was hardly able to pick up her infant child at all. A young mother unable to enjoy the pleasure and comfort of picking up and holding her first child. Doesn't that sound more compelling than simply a young woman being in an accident and being "limited in her activities?" Talking to your clients and the people involved will spring tidbits of personal information that you can use in your work. Utilizing words to describe all of the senses; what one sees, hears, touches, smells, tastes and intuitively "feels." Capturing the moment, the look in an eye, the feel of a breeze, the taste of a poison, will spring to life a happening. This method will also bring people "alive" and make them more memorable to the person reading the demand or letter.

This carries us to what will likely take up another sizeable portion of your time—interviewing and gathering facts from your clients and witnesses. The journalistic foundation of who, what, where, when, and why forms a solid foundation for your fact-finding missions. Going a couple of steps further, you could ask open-ended questions, such as:

*Tell me about how the accident happened, in your own words? (rather than, did the accident happen at 6 p.m. on a dark street? Let the client or witness fill in the blanks) What happened next?*

*How did you feel when you first found out about the extent of your injuries?*

*How did your family feel?*

*How did they cope?*

*How has this incident changed your day-to-day activities?*

*What do you see for your future as far as your physical capabilities?*

In summary, getting the facts is fundamental, but probing deeper into the abyss of human thoughts and emotions will glean treasures buried below the surface, and also possibly give you, the client, and your attorney an advantage in resolving the case.

How do I know these tactics really work? Noticeably, in addition to the rock-solid answer of obtaining rapid, unproblematic settlements, and having happy clients, and satisfied lawyers, I asked those whose job it is to evaluate some of these persuasive documents, such as demand letters. A seasoned insurance adjuster I knew told me that threading personal information and telling how an accident or incident really affected someone's everyday life truly brought the severity and "humanness" out. It made him understand the impact on someone's life clearer. And, ultimately, it made him settle the case quicker and for more value because they know that the "story" will touch and influence a jury. I have also asked attorneys and they relay that they too, like their interest piqued, and appreciate the time it took someone to hunt down the details of a slice of someone's life that somehow went awry.

From time to time while I was working at the personal injury law firm, my boss would take on a few criminal, probate or divorce cases and I had to work those as well. I learned how to brush up on different, unfamiliar areas of the law, where to look for the special forms these areas of law require and also, how to ask questions depending on the matter at hand. If I did not know a specific procedure, I would call the clerk of court or court administrator and ask, or I would ask one of my paralegal friends in other firms.

Retaining expert witnesses may also be a part of your job. Sometimes the single way to show a court something, to get a certain fact or set of facts in front of a court, or the only way to make your argument relevant, is to have a disinterested outsider with some advanced knowledge testify as to "expert" areas of your argument, areas outside of the realm of the standard layperson; thus, they may be qualified as an "expert witness." This usually is a very interesting project and forces you to be resourceful and well-rounded as a paralegal. I recall trying to find an expert in something really obscure, like growing some sort of exotic orchids. The reason we needed an expert in this particular case was a divorce case where the opposing spouse, the husband, was a botanist who showed and grew these orchids, but claimed no money was made or could be made from them. We needed an expert who could testify that, in fact, a specialized orchid grower could make a substantial sum of money, as was the wife's position. Well, after scouring the yellow pages and internet, and finding nothing, I started calling local garden clubs and perusing planting journals at the local university until I hit pay dirt! A grower of the exotic orchids! I contacted her and she became our very valuable expert witness.

As stated before, and as I learned first-hand, probably the most central skill you will need to get a grip on first and keep a hold of is case management, because this will dictate what you do, and when you'll do it. Even if you have to make five lists, keep three calendars and go through the file cabinets monthly, you will need to calendar everything and keep up with the deadlines. In essence you will learn to "look after" your boss when it comes to deadlines. You will need to prioritize for him or her and remind, remind, remind. Then, you may need to nag sometimes when they don't listen too attentively.

Several of the legal assistants I know have become so good at their jobs and so efficient that their attorneys become, well, comfortable (read: spoiled). They rely so heavily on their assistant to remind them of deadlines and to tell them what needs to be done that the tables have been completely turned as to who should be calling the shots. Oftentimes, the legal assistant knows more about the status of the cases than the attorney! This can be a very flattering, but dangerous thing to happen. The attorney should always know what is happening on his or her cases and be the one to conduct the course of the case, and should always make the crucial, case-relevant decisions.

Unfortunately, getting attorneys to comply with this can be difficult, sometimes even impossible. They are often so busy in their professional and personal lives, so very regimented and locked down every hour of every day, including weekends, that they must rely on others heavily, almost exclusively, for support.

This is wonderful from a legal assisting viewpoint, and certainly, this is how the field of legal assisting became so popular, but your boss is still the attorney, after all, and responsible for their own actions as well as their legal assistants' and staff's actions. Most importantly, the attorney's career and reputation, and his or her license to practice law, rests on the attorney's devotion to zealously and competently representing the interests of the client above all.

How to strike a good balance and keep the office, clients and work flowing smoothly?

## BUILDING A RAPPORT WITH YOUR BOSS

Communication is key between you and your attorney and usually regularly scheduled status conferences or meetings with your boss will help the case management process along, and give him or her a snapshot of the status of the open cases in your office.

At the personal injury law firm, my week usually began with a reminder and overview session.

"A response to the Defendant's motion to dismiss is due. The hearing is next week. And the pre-trial conference on the Smith case is 35 days away—any more discovery or motions needed?" I would typically ask my boss. Thinking ahead is a key factor in a law office.

He would invariably respond, "Okay, but do me a favor? If I haven't done it by Wednesday, please remind me again."

And I would have to remind him again—attorneys are almost constantly busy, and various fires needing to be put out would arise and my Monday morning reminder would be forgotten almost as soon as I made it. I also make it a habit to write down everything that may seem pertinent, even minimally. This is a cardinal rule that I have come to live by: write *everything* down, even the tiniest detail. You will never be able to remember every little facet of information and will definitely need the information and little nuances later on, especially weeks or months later. You can even create a notes file for each case to keep track of your notes and reminders, in case an opposing attorney's assistant or a county clerk can't recall speaking with you, and you need to remind him or her of a certain conversation, filing or event. I carry a notepad with me almost everywhere I go. I also learned that it was helpful to my overall sense of organization, if an attorney asked to see me, that I would automatically bring a notepad and pen to write whatever they needed down, or take simple notes to add to the file for later review.

Getting to know your attorney takes time and is like any other relationship. If it is built on mutual trust, respect and courtesy, it should flourish. If not, it will likely crumble.

Every attorney is different. Some like a close relationship with their assistants, talking about their weekends, sharing happy hours now and then, and seeking their personal feedback on cases. Others are strictly businesslike and do not wish to get too close, personally, with their staff. Whichever type, or in-between variation, of lawyer you wind up assigned to, it is best to respect their wishes as much as you can within your own paradigm of organizational structure. I once knew a legal assistant who was chatty, outgoing and extremely extroverted—a real "people person." This social butterfly was paired with an all-business, no-frills, somewhat stuffy lawyer who liked to keep things strictly professional. Well, as might be expected, their personality styles clashed and from the first day of working together got along poorly at best. He thought she was flighty and too loose with personal and case information, and she thought he was a stereotypically formal dud, until they each got reassigned.

Likewise, once I was assigned to a new attorney who was nothing but fun and games, with every day like walking into a boyish frat party. Oh sure, this was great for a while—a short while! But soon I tired of always looking after him, trying to pin him down to sign anything, covering for him when he didn't show up for hearings and depositions, and making every excuse in the book for when he was out on the golf course. Finally, our boss also grew weary of his sketchy work ethic and had a serious talk with him before the behavior went any further and could potentially damage the reputation of the firm.

Anyway, try to feel out how your attorney likes to work and give it a chance, and bend your ideals a bit to accommodate his or her likes, dislikes, and idiosyncrasies, even if they may at times feel unnatural. A good working relationship should incorporate elements from both individuals, akin to a metallic alloy, and as far as personality conflicts run, most attorneys are very nice, interesting people and do actually care about their legal assistants' lives, both inside and outside of the office.

Other considerations to be aware of may include items such as, is your attorney a morning or afternoon person? Do they favor morning or afternoon appointments? Does he or she prefer to limit the number of appointments per day? Do they want the two hours prior to a hearing blocked off and all their calls held? Does he or she usually like to work under pressure, or possibly, procrastinate until something has to be done, or do they like keeping up with the work methodically, to the best of their abilities? Does your boss have family obligations on certain days or nights that might impact his or her productivity or effectiveness at the office? Are they married? Have kids? All these things, and more, may affect how you handle scheduling for your attorney and the flow of the work in your particular office or firm.

This bonding between attorney and assistant will of course take time, but learning more of these personal traits and characteristics can allow you to build a solid camaraderie and ultimately better share your routines at the office.

# DIFFERENT AREAS OF LAW AND THEIR WORK

The actual work you do will depend on which area or practice you work. The majority of law firms utilize their legal assistants for summarizing records and depositions, drafting correspondence, retaining expert witnesses, drafting motions and orders, maintaining files, case management, scheduling and client contact. But there are some specific features to each particular area of law, that one would likely not know about unless one had first-hand experience. Having been through these experiences, I have compiled several of those distinctions and I will let you "sneak a peek" into some first-hand knowledge and tips I have learned, which have greatly helped with some of the more popular, distinct areas of law. Of course, all areas of the law are not delved into here, as I have not worked personally in every area. You will find, though, that many areas of law can tend to overlap each other. For example, a divorce or family law client might need assistance selling their marital home, which may well necessitate referral to a real estate attorney, either outsourced, or in another section of the firm, or perhaps they need assistance or a legal opinion on updating their wills, which is squarely a probate and estate planning matter.

# FAMILY LAW

If you work in a family law firm, it is good advice to have a box of tissues on your desk at all times. Most family law cases will require a saint's quantity of patience, and the ability to sometimes act as a minor crisis counselor. With family law, prior to weekends, especially holidays, and before every summer vacation, get ready for the customary onslaught of visitation dilemmas and crises. Invariably, one spouse will refuse to drop off and/or pick up their mutual child, or is late, early, wants more time, less time or will not allow visitation with the child/children until the other spouse pays the outstanding support that is owed. You will, if you work in this field, see your share of marriages that are abusive for various reasons, and may end up with the opinion that some parents simply should not be permitted to raise children. Despite the seemingly sad circumstances and heated debates, family law can be very rewarding. Many legal assistants believe that it gives one a feeling of nobility to help someone, especially children, get out of an atrocious situation and seek a better life with at least some guarantee of protection from harm.

With the emotional tribulations of divorce and other aspects of family law, you will plainly see that many of these individuals have an inability to rationally discuss and agree to what needs to be done to remedy their particular dysfunction, which is the reason they have sought counsel, and badly need to get out of their unhappy circumstances, and find their happiness and satisfaction elsewhere.

Mostly, the divorce side of this area of law deals with gathering financial information regarding assets and liabilities, and trying to divvy up the totality of property, which may also include investments, retirement accounts, annuities, and the like, equitably between the husband and wife. Alimony, child visitation and support are also substantial issues that you will run into in the practice of family law, and it will help you to become familiar with your state's statutes regarding family law. Other work you will likely be exposed to if your attorney practices in the area of family law include modifications, such as when a former spouse seeks to modify, or change, child support, visitation, alimony, or another aspect of the final judgment or decree of divorce, and contempt and enforcement matters. Hearings of this type intend to show the court that a party has either done something they shouldn't, or hasn't done something they should, and ask the court to force the other spouse to pay, or perform another required action. Other components of family law, outside of the scope of this discussion, might include adoptions, abandonment, separate maintenance, surrogacy issues, dependency matters, termination of parental rights, and various other issues as may be accepted in your state.

As a paralegal in a family law firm, you will most likely prepare initial pleadings and documents, such as the Petition for Dissolution of Marriage, which is the formal document asking the court for a divorce, assist in obtaining service of process upon the other spouse, prepare and keep track of discovery such as interrogatories, requests for production and requests for admissions, schedule depositions and mediations, and if needed, ultimately, prepare for a trial. You may also keep the filing up to date and the files organized and have a good amount of client contact. In summary, a good form file, patience and people skills, and knowledge of the family law rules of civil procedure, especially for service of process, deadlines, and default issues, will be important things to master in this field. One of your biggest allies in the family law theater may be an experienced process server to serve hostile, or to find missing, spouses.

Client service is very important in this area of law. How to further go the extra mile for your clients beyond doing a solid job for them? The simple answer: care for them as people, and treat them as you would wish to be treated if you were involved in a similarly deplorable situation. A suggested way to do this would be to compile a list of resources such as local abused or battered spouse shelters, job assistance counselors, single parent support groups, co-parent coordinators, and divorce support groups. A little digging to find and organize these local support systems into a listing or even a booklet to give to those who need them or seek them, will be vastly consoling and reassuring to many of your attorney's clients— just be sure to check with your attorney and/or state or local bar association for any special rules governing booklets or brochures.

I really enjoyed working in family law; in fact, it is one of my favorite areas of law. Most of the forms you will use these days are standard, that is, they come straight from the Rules of Civil or Family Law Procedure, statutes, or the state's Supreme Court and are the same ones everyone uses, or in substantial conformity with the rules. Also, as family law matters, if they go to trial, are heard only by a judge and not by a jury, I also like not having to deal with jury trials, which necessitate jury instructions and voir dire questions.

# PERSONAL INJURY

Personal Injury and Insurance Defense law can also be rewarding and very interesting. The cases will run the gamut, from devastating injuries in a car accident to an innocent diner cutting his tongue on a piece of glass in a fast-food burger to a crestfallen family with a bedsore-ridden senior member in a decrepit, understaffed nursing home. As with any area of law, being a good listener is an important trait in this arena, but perhaps more so with personal injury, as great detail and inquiry must be made in order to prohibit prior circumstances or injuries from negatively impacting the client's case. You must be able to listen to a lot of emotionally charged opinions, and tie them into the facts to spotlight the real issues. You must also deal with people's motivations, i.e., monetary gain, and expectations of their case. People skills are essential in working in personal injury, medical malpractice, and nursing home cases, especially if you work on the plaintiff's side. You must also learn to tactfully, but purposefully, dig a little deeper into people's backgrounds such as prior injuries, prior health problems, and general character, which may become an issue at trial, and will help you prepare your attorney if a client displays an otherwise unwholesome opinion, propensity or trait—it is much better for the lawyer to find out these characteristics *before* going to trial than *during* the trial, believe me! Also, this is a perfect area to couple your interest with the type of law you do. If you like medical jargon or digging into issues of liability (who is at fault) and damages (injuries), then you will probably do well in personal injury or medical malpractice law.

This is the area of law in which I have the most experience, and I have performed work on every aspect of the case, from intake and inception to final closing statements during a trial and appeal. I have sat in on client intakes (usually the first meeting with a new or potentially new client), compiled pre-suit information such as insurance information, and medical records and written demand letters to insurance adjusters, who are typically assigned as the insurance company liaison on a case or claim. In litigation, that is, when a case cannot be settled and a lawsuit has been filed, I have drafted and prepared complaints, obtained service on defendants, prepared, responded to and tracked discovery, coordinated and scheduled depositions, mediations and trials, and prepared for trials. I also had heavy client contact; actually, I met with clients almost more than my attorney did, which you may find is common in high volume personal injury practices with a large caseload.

I especially enjoyed preparing a file for mediation, such as compiling and confirming medical specials (these are medical bills, wage loss information and the like—basically everything monetary incurred as a result of an accident or incident.) I also savor the hypothetical of envisioning how a case, controversy, or argument would play in front of a jury. Jury trials are the major ingredient and variable in this type of law, and it is important to always think about someday being before a jury with the information you are seeking or have obtained. I was always fond of analyzing a set of facts and trying to think up every possible way a person may interpret the facts. Then, I would usually discuss with my boss how to counteract any negative emotions, or feelings those facts may conjure up. Basically, we would try to think up worst-case scenarios and "head them off at the pass" or try to address the problem in the light most favorable to our client.

If you encounter a case with some hurdles to overcome, say a client with pre-existing injuries, with those injuries aggravated by a recent car accident, the need for educating the jury about these injuries and the status both before and after the accident, preparing your client for testimony and obtaining an experienced expert is crucial. I used to mentally dissect our clients with these types of complaints, looking for believability, background and/or tendency to exaggerate. In front of a jury panel, there are only a certain number of possible scenarios that jurors could reasonably find: a) believe the client was injured as a direct result of the accident, and believe in the injuries and damages therefrom, and award relief or money recovery, b) believe the client was injured as a direct result of the accident but *not* believe the injuries are severe enough to warrant recovery, c) not believe your client was injured in the accident, yet still believe your client's injuries—perhaps they think it was from another unrelated incident or accident, or d) not believe any of it, and award an outright defense verdict. There are also hybrids of these that jurors could potentially wrestle with. It is important to create strategies and contingent plans for dealing with "b", "c", and "d", as only "a" would result in a monetary award and only "a" would seem to be the ideal plaintiff's outcome.

Defending such cases, known formally as insurance defense, is also all about compiling medical records and bills, deciphering prior injuries, accidents, etc., assessing your own client, the Defendant, and his or her background, and essentially trying to poke holes in or tear apart the Plaintiff's case, and point the finger away from the insurance company's insured. Unfortunately, having worked in Plaintiff's firms for many years, I know that Plaintiffs can be their own worst enemies and sometimes the defense is hardly even needed to try to attack a Plaintiff's character and background. If a Plaintiff does not disclose something like a past accident, past injuries, or even personal information like prior lawsuits, and the defense finds out—and they do have wily and craftily successful methods of finding out this type of mistake, omission, or misrepresentation—this may haunt the case sooner or later, either with a decreased or even rescinded offer from the defendant at mediation, or worse yet, when the Plaintiff is before a jury. In other words, if you and your attorney *know* about your client's damaging issues, you can better analyze the situation and conduct damage control before it is too late and a jury has returned an unfavorable verdict to the client.

There's an old saying in personal injury law that I have heard from several attorneys, assistants and practitioners, that, "It is not the Defense who wins cases, it is the Plaintiff who loses them." From the many, many years working in plaintiff's personal injury law, I find this statement to be universally true and is why excellent communications and meaningful client contact are your best weapons against such events. Don't forget that much of the practice of law, especially trial law, is one side or the other having to meet certain "burdens." These burdens are crucial to proving up a case or not, and a defendant does not have to disprove anything; if the plaintiff has failed to prove his case or meet his or her burden, the defense will win with what is called a directed verdict. It is absolutely integral that the plaintiff's case be proven, affirmatively and absolutely, to prevent a directed, or defense, verdict, and a *very* unhappy client.

In personal injury matters, if you are the Plaintiff's side, you generally do not get paid until a case settles, or a win at trial is obtained. A contingency fee contract usually rules in these situations and means that your firm will collect a percentage of the gross settlement. What this means to you as a paralegal is volume and lots of work! If you are close to your attorney and he or she discloses to you the monthly quota or intake necessary to maintain the firm or practice, you can strive to meet and exceed it. Just a brief hypothetical—if we—myself and the rest of a law firm's staff—knew we needed $30,000 per month to meet our overhead, we knew that meant settling about four or five low-value cases per month or one larger-value case. To do that, we had to make sure we had at least a couple of demands per week finalized and out in the mail, and schedule at least five media-tions per month, as a large percentage of these cases settle at mediation, but you could always count on one or two not settling, and moving forward towards the inevitability of trial.

For defense attorneys and paralegals, the name of the game is billable time. This is how defense firms make their overhead—they get paid a fee by the insurance companies to defend matters, and must keep track of the time they spend on a particular case, which expenditures will be reviewed from time to time by the adjuster assigned to the case. Learn to meticulously keep track of your time, your work, and bill appropriately.

In summary, for either side of personal injury, build and maintain a good form file, and pay special attention to the Rules of Civil Procedure regarding discovery, scheduling, motions, etc. Also, find out from your attorney or other legal assis-tants what the rules in your state are regarding insurance coverage, the statutes thereon, and "stacking," or other coverage issues which might be beneficial to you in setting up an organizational inquiry of a file. Each state and district can have different and sometimes quite particular rules and regulations, so try to learn your local nuances as soon as you can. Creating a good trial checklist is very use-ful, as is compiling a list of trial resources, such as legal exhibit preparation serv-ices, video services, and trial consultant services.

# BANKRUPTCY

Bankruptcy law is another area where you must deal with people facing tough decisions in their lives. The stress that finances have on a family can sometimes be devastating to their interfamilial relationships. Having a good database of support resources for your bankruptcy clients is essential to giving them service that is not expected and will make those clients appreciate your and your firm's efforts on their behalf.

For example, my former boss used to do quite a bit of bankruptcy work for debtors (those filing bankruptcy) and used to really take the time with them, at the intake phase to sift through what was the real reason behind the need for the bankruptcy. Was it separation or divorce? Medical bills due to unexpected or dev-astating illness? Was it simply bad planning and overextending on credit cards? Or a classic debt abuser, running up astronomical debt only to try and shirk responsibility? He would find this out and refer them, if needed, to credit coun-seling centers, marriage counseling, and other support centers in our town who could help them through this financial crisis. He would also maintain a list of companies who were willing to extend credit to bankrupt individuals to try to get clients in contact with those who could help them make a fresh start after bank-ruptcy hung an albatross around their neck. Believe me, some lawyers simply ask for the "financials"—plug in the numbers and spit out a bankruptcy petition without delving into the real reasons. But those attorneys and staff who take the extra time to help the people behind the cases, will likely "hook" a client for life, and get referral business out of the thankful client.

Oftentimes, clients seek attorneys to help fix a major problem in their lives, a problem they cannot fix on their own. Going the extra mile can help people do just that, and show them some dignity in the process.

As a paralegal, you will need to know the difference between the different types of bankruptcies. Briefly, the major types are Chapter 7 and Chapter 13. Chapter 7 bankruptcies deal with total liquidation, meaning, the selling off of all assets to pay liabilities and creditors. Chapter 13 bankruptcies deal with the court ordering a restructuring plan or schedule, as in working out payment plans to lower monthly payments, or lowering the total debt overall. There are other types also, such as Chapter 11, all based off of the United States Bankruptcy Code, but I have never dealt with or worked on any of them personally, but a good course in bankruptcy law, likely offered at a local community college or university, should arm you with this knowledge.

You will also be preparing schedules of financial information and tracking cases through discharge, or completion. Most bankruptcy attorneys I know these days have a special computer program to input the financial information and churn out the required schedules and documents. Client contact is also heavy in this area of law, and again, this section of law is all about volume. This means you will be busy, busy, busy! But it is also gratifying to help people through very stressful times.

One final thought. Bankruptcy falls under Federal Law, so bone up on federal procedure and rules, and obtain a copy of the local rules in your district by con-tacting the clerk's office for a copy. These days, you may even be able to download them off of the Internet.

# CRIMINAL LAW

I had the pleasure of working on criminal law cases during my years as a legal assistant and also while assisting my husband in building our business.

This huge and dynamic area of the law is also rewarding from a constitu-tional and personal liberty standpoint, and certainly has the element of high stakes. No longer dealing primarily with money like most civil cases (except in cases where monetary restitution is also made or sought), a criminal case is where the defendant is charged with a crime by the State, the prosecuting agency in most jurisdictions, with the direct and proximate potential that someone's life and liberty will be, "on the line" in the form of jail or prison time as a punishment. The Federal government can also bring charges against someone and these are initiated by the United States Attorney's Office.

Another reality is that for each crime or alleged crime, there is a victim, so sometimes the victim or their family has faced or will face devastation, in the form of harm to themselves or a loved one, which can make for touchy and emotionally charged courtrooms, especially at sentencing hearings. I have only worked on the defense side of criminal law, but I do know paralegals who have worked at the state attorney's, or district attorney's office, and the U.S. Attorney's Office. These paralegals assist in prosecuting cases.

For either side, you must learn discovery procedures, compile witness and exhibit information and coordinate depositions, as well as notices of alibi, where the defendant claims to have been in a different place at the time the alleged crime was being committed, which alibi is usually supported by the eyewitness testimony of one or more individuals. Often there will be heard a suppression hearing, where the defense attorney tries to show the court that certain aspects of the arrest, search, or seizure were illegal or without cause, and the resulting evidence obtained must or should be suppressed, or not permitted into evidence at trial. A successful suppression hearing will almost always result in the prosecuting agency dropping or dismissing the charges, as the evidence suppressed was likely crucial to them meeting their burden of proving guilt beyond a reasonable doubt (see, there are those pesky burdens again!).

Trial work, including jury trials, are a crucial aspect of criminal law, as many cases actually go to trial. This is also a perfect area of law for the legal assistant to marry their personal interests to either fight for the government and victim's side or to fight for the rights of inmates and those accused of crimes. Post-judgment work, such as criminal appeals and post-conviction motions are a large part of criminal trial work as well, although some attorneys do not directly handle criminal appeals, choosing rather to refer these matters out to appellate experts in their field.

A common question people ask when talking about criminal law is, "Do you ever represent someone who you know is guilty?" Well, of course we do. Actually, it has been my experience that the majority of people arrested know what they did, know what they did was wrong, realize the mistake, and want to pay for their actions, but also want to obtain a fair deal. Whether or not a client is guilty usually does not enter into the equation when an attorney makes the decision to represent that client—that person's fundamental constitutional right is to have representation to the best ability of the attorney, if they can afford one, or one will be provided in most cases if they cannot.

For example, I recall one of my husband's clients was accused of driving under the influence (DUI or DWI in some states), with property damage, as she ran a red light and hit another car—luckily, no one was injured, but she pretty much destroyed two vehicles in the process. In this case it wasn't alcohol that was the offending substance, but an abuse and near overdose of prescription drugs. The client had submitted to blood and breath analysis, so the state had clear and convincing evidence of her impairment. Clearly, from the videotape we obtained through discovery, she was impaired—she stumbled around, slurred her speech, danced around, and laughed uncontrollably when the officers asked her to perform field sobriety exercises. She knew that she was impaired, or should have known it, and knew she had a problem with pills, which she candidly admitted to her attorney. He advised her of the highly improbable chance of suppressing the videotape or the blood analysis evidence, which had been gathered using approved methodology and by trained personnel on recently calibrated equipment, and that if a jury were to view the tape and hear of the drugs she had taken, which is an almost regular occurrence in criminal cases of this nature, she would almost surely be convicted. Further, as DUI with property damage has escalated penalties and fines, including up to a year in jail, she had a tough decision to make. The attorney changed her not guilty plea to one of guilty in her best interest, after consultation and at her request, and pled "open" to the court to allow her to enter a residential substance abuse program, in lieu of jail time. The outcome? This time, she completed the program, paid off all her fines, court costs, and cleaned herself up. We never heard from her again, and must hopefully assume that she is leading a much happier, and healthier, life.

"Have you ever represented someone knowing they weren't guilty?" is the tandem to the former question, asked almost as frequently.

I distinctly recall a middle-aged, gentle, well-spoken man whom from the moment I first saw him I knew could not have stolen anything at all, let alone premeditated and planned to break into a vehicle with burglary tools, bypassing a security system in the process, stealing money, guns, and expensive stereo equipment, as he had been accused of. Upon investigation, there was absolutely no evidence to support the State's theory—no direct evidence at all. No fingerprints, no burglary tools recovered, no marks on the vehicle showing forcible entry, no true eyewitnesses, no items from the vehicle recovered in the possession of the client, no…anything! So why did the prosecutors pursue this case? They claimed to have a witness, not an *eye*witness, but an individual who said he saw someone "suspicious" in the area of the crime, although he could not elucidate what about the individual was suspicious. This very general description ("white male, between thirty and forty-five, between 150 and 200 pounds, no distinguishing marks or features") vaguely matched our client, the middle aged man, who happened to be out for a stroll in his neighborhood (albeit at least several blocks away from where the crime occurred), where he had lived all his life. He was married, with two young teenagers, was a computer network engineer for a large multi-national telecommunications company, and had never had so much as a speeding ticket. This seemed absolutely ludicrous, and a gross abuse of prosecutorial discretion and taxpayer resources! That man was so adamant about not being anywhere near this car, the area of the car, and didn't have a need or desire to steal anything. But this poor man, placed under the microscope for several months prior to his trial, had to agonize over the situation, the trial, and the possibility that he might be convicted and go to prison.

Unfortunately, the State took this all the way to jury trial, refusing to drop the charges, deal, or plea the case. The client, overcome with emotion, broke down in a torrent of tears when he took the stand at trial. The state lost the trial, resoundingly so— so much that the Judge suggested the man retain a civil attorney to look into a civil action against the State. Thankfully, the jury saw the true character of this man, believed his alibi, and found him not guilty. And, as a service to him, for free, my boss arranged to do the paperwork to have his arrest and case expunged, so that none of it would appear on his record. It was a difficult and stressful situation, but with a happy ending.

As a paralegal in the criminal field, you may have strong feelings about a situation or person one way or the other, but you must sometimes place them aside and perform the task at hand, your job. People skills are also essential as you will be dealing with extraordinary emotions, as well as their family members and even the media from time to time, such as on high-profile cases. Volume also dictates in a criminal law practice, as well as case management and trial preparation skills. You will probably go to trial much more in a criminal practice than say, a personal injury practice, so a good trial checklist and trial resource list tailored to your attorney's requests and requirements would bode extremely well.

# MUSIC AND ENTERTAINMENT LAW

Finally, in working with my husband in the music and entertainment legal world, I have learned about passion and perseverance. Passion for a vision and for the craft or art of your client. Perseverance to see and make happen an apparent long-shot transform into a viable record deal, book deal, or the like. If you are lucky enough to work in this active and creative field, you must keep up with the industry. Anyone who works or even knows a little about the music and entertainment world knows trends come and go and who's hot today is out tomorrow. This is where reading trade magazines and publications, checking web sites for chart toppers and generally being plugged into the "biz" will make you shine.

As stated previously, and as you have learned in this book, you can almost always find the right fit with an area of law and your personality and interests. If you are interested in the music, publishing, or entertainment world, this area of law is the Utopia of that theory. I must admit, I like the perks, such as free concert and sporting event tickets, backstage passes, dinners at new clubs, seeing your client on MTV, and hoping that your clients are the next big thing and being able to be a part of making their dreams happen. Your people skills will also be able to be heavily used to deal with lots of different types or personalities from managers to agents to artists. Yes, and with those people sometimes come the egos, the divas and the "rock stars," and ulterior, sometimes salacious motives and attitudes—this comes with the territory. My personal experience is that if an "unknown" comes through the door with an already out of control attitude and mediocre talent, they will remain, perhaps thankfully, "unknown." However, those who keep their egos in check, build upon their talent, focus on their goal and keep at their craft, usually amount to something. Even the biggest dreams can be played out in small ways and still be achieved, i.e., a band playing a local club with their eye on playing a stadium in five years, or the author who has her book self-published and sells 2,000 copies, but with her vision of doubling sales for her next novel, and the next and the next.

Most of the attorneys I know in this area of law are sole practitioners or are partners in or work in smaller, or what are commonly known as "boutique" firms. In the entertainment field, the predominance of attorneys are in the music meccas—New York City, Los Angeles, Nashville, and to a lesser extent, Miami. In most other areas, music and entertainment law is a niche section of law and requires knowledge of the local scene and tightly knit music, literary and arts community in order to be a valid and prosperous area in which to practice.

First, the legal assistant in the entertainment field should know the nuts and bolts —the legal issues you will likely encounter. High on that list is the knowledge that contractual interpretation and negotiation, of a highly specialized and particular nature, are the crux of this area of law, along with copyrights, royalties, publishing rights, and intellectual property law. Some of the more important would include:

Copyrights—Artists may insure themselves maximum protection and recourse should their material be infringed upon if they register their material with the U.S. Library of Congress Copyright Office; however, registration is not required in order for an artist or author to claim a copyright in a work, as is commonly mistaken. An artist or author can claim a common law copyright simply when his or her material is fixed in a tangible medium, which could be writing out sheet music, or recording the song to a cassette tape or compact disc, or in some other physical form. However, registration grants the highest form of infringement protection, and affords the author statutory damages and attorney's fees upon a proper showing of infringement, among other extra "goodies," and is strongly recommended. Few attorneys would recommend to trust an artist's creative output to the so-called 'poor man's copyright.' Infringement happens, and actually happens quite frequently, and an author of a work wants to have the utmost in protection available—and that is a proper registration of their work, which also constitutes requisite notice under the Copyright Act of 1976, as amended.

Royalties—Retail Sales Royalties, in the parlance of the music business, consist of the percentage of the suggested U.S. retail list price of the album that the artist receives from their record company, minus any deductions (called "recoupment" or "recouping costs") such as recording costs, costs of a producer, marketing, advertising, and sometimes even video production costs, and any other monies spent on behalf of the artist on the exploitation and promotion of their record.

Publishing—One of the more convoluted areas of music law; in a nutshell, when a record company presses and sells an artist's intellectual property resident on the label's property, the physical disc itself, it must pay a statutory *publishing* royalty to the artist. This right flowed necessarily from the literary counterpart of book publishing—that, when a writer authors a book, the book publisher must pay the author a royalty every time it copies the book. The statutory royalty for music, which increases incrementally as set by Congress, currently stands at $.08 per song of up to five minutes. It may not sound like much, but it sure can add up in a hurry, especially if the artist hits sales echelons of gold or platinum, 500,000 and 1,000,000 respectively. Record labels regularly use freedom to contract as a way around statutory royalties, however. Major labels and their cadre of trained, specialized attorneys are crafty and efficient at coming up with creative ways around statutory requirements, which is why an artist needs a trained and experienced attorney to negotiate their contract or deal.

The top three services requested by my husband's clients are to, "shop recordings to record labels, review contracts from record companies, publishers, managers, etc., and help resolve disputes involving other band members, managers, producers, etc."

Knowing this, a paralegal can do much to assist his or her attorney in the practice of music law. First, since contracts are a huge part of the work in this field, one should bone up on contract law and at least know the basics of offer, acceptance, consideration, deal memos, letters of inducement and loan-out letters, along with more in depth music law topics such as progressive term and option clauses, the gamut of royalty clauses one might expect to find, auditing provisions, and "controlled composition" clauses, all of which are somewhat complex and outside of the scope of this book. One way to be advantageous is to create and maintain a super-organized form and "clause" template file. For example, in a recording contract, there is always the standard minimum recording obligation clause. Sometimes there are clauses dealing with touring and merchandising. Maintaining a database of these clauses, and others typically used in music law contracts, along with much of the standard "boilerplate" you have seen in other contracts (severability clauses, choice of forum, indemnifications, and warranties, to name a few) will aid you in putting together a good working draft contract tailored to the client's needs, fast and efficiently, and which will be a great assistance to the attorney.

Be sure to keep plugged into the biz, because as in hemlines and hairstyles, things change in an *American Idol* heartbeat. Read the trade publications, such as *Music Connection* Magazine. Attend your local bar association's CLE seminars on entertainment topics, especially the caselaw update seminars, which can be crucial in helping to issue spot on current hot-button issues.

## FINAL THOUGHTS

Some final thoughts to consider are that there are also many different types of structure to law offices and environments where paralegals work beyond the large firm vs. small firm debate. Large firms tend to hire, for the most part, only experienced workers. Small firms tend to give you more responsibility and are usually willing to take more of a chance on someone less experienced, although they generally do not pay as well, and usually do not offer as comprehensive of a benefit plan as the mid to large sized firms.

Also, some, especially larger, law firms or agencies are "task oriented" and have their legal assistants do just one task, such as discovery, or retaining experts and keeping those experts up to date, while others subscribe to the "jack of all trades" theory and have their paralegals doing everything and anything, even filing, copying, and running things to the courthouse when needed.

Those who are administrative paralegals work in usually state or government sponsored or funded legal service programs, as counselors or advocates and may assist their clients in obtaining government or other types of benefits. Administrative paralegals generally have the freedom, and the accountability of maintaining their own caseloads, with total responsibility from beginning to end. Some may also represent clients at various administrative agency proceedings.

Other paralegals work in county, circuit, or federal courthouses, or directly for the government or one of its agencies, such as for the Federal Trade Commission, or Justice Department. According to the National Federation of Paralegal Associations, these paralegals generally collect and evaluate evidence, conduct hearings, draft proposed legislation, and answer inquiries pertaining to federal laws and regulations.

Additionally, the United States Military hires paralegals to assist in working within their military system and tribunals.

If you enjoy teaching, you may even use your knowledge and skills to teach the next generation of legal assistants.

Take a minute to ask yourself—do you do well in office politics and are you a team player? Are you comfortable working in a department or performing a specific task, such as discovery, day in and day out? If so, a large firm may be for you.

On the other hand, do you like more variety and having your hand in all aspects of a case? Are you extremely self-sufficient and can work with little supervision? Then, a smaller or medium sized firm may be your ticket.

Or, you may be a political enthusiast who thrives in such an entwined environment and who wishes to have a hand in drafting legislation or working for the government.

No matter what type of law firm or company you work for, the overall theme I aspire to convey is that you will have a chance of make a difference in people's lives and you can find the right fit for yourself, one that will give you great pleasure. You will have a chance to see and hear extremely intimate details of people's lives and assist these clients in remedying a situation to which they have no solution. Of course, everything you do in a case is confidential and intimate details or any detail should never be disclosed so as to breach confidentiality rules. Even my specific examples in this book have been altered for any identifying characteristics so as not to breach anybody's or any firm's privacy and confidentiality. But seeing a large portion of the intimate details of people's lives and thoughts may help you, personally, become a well-rounded person and learn about people and what makes them tick.

Such as, what really motivates people to commit crimes and do harm to others?
Why do people want to sue?
Why do people not want to pay when they know they are wrong?
What are people's real motives and what makes them feel a certain way?
What exactly does "justice" mean to people?
These are all philosophical questions that you can seek answers to by working in the legal field. Rare is the profession where you have access to people's medical records, criminal records, employment records, tax records, and various other very personal records. And while all of this may be interesting, you must always

respect people's private lives and *never, ever* reveal names and identifying characteristics. But it sure is fascinating and gives you much insight into the human personality!

I recall a man we represented who was in a horrendous car crash where the other driver died. The deceased driver was clearly at fault having driven across the median of a highway into the opposite lanes. The offer to settle the case was substantial, in the hundreds of thousands of dollars, being that our client sustained a severe injury requiring several surgeries and medical treatment for years. The monetary offer to settle was decent and we probably could have bettered it without filing a lawsuit in court. The client, though, believed that, "They can't get away with this!" "They" being the company who employed the dead man and who owned the vehicle. This insurance carrier of the company would cover our client for the accident. Well, our client, "Wanted to sue and call the TV stations and cry to a jury about what they did to me!" He was going beyond "principles and justice;" he was getting vindictive and was out for revenge. It was not even completely about the money—this man wanted to tell his story to any who would listen, and make sure the actions were never repeated, and for that he wanted publicity. But justice means different things to different people. It may mean money, or someone going to jail, a highly public trial against a huge corporation, or even a simple apology.

You will find that people react to situations different ways. Some feel wronged and want the whole world to know it. They want to punish a tortfeasor (a person who is at fault) for more than they really should be punished.

As I have stated before, you will learn about people's motives, gain insight into the human psyche, and why people do certain things. I found out, in time, that this man's marriage was crumbling at the same time and he had financial problems unrelated to this accident. He blamed the accident on all of his problems and blamed the company for his injuries *and* everything else happening in his life. Of course, an accident is an upheaval in anyone's life, and certainly can exacerbate other life problems, but we always tried to counsel people to keep things in perspective.

One senior partner I worked with was excellent about gently advising clients to put their cases out of their minds. He used to tell them to live their lives as they would if they did not have a pending case and the weight would eventually be lifted. Numerous clients over the years have told me that this simple philosophy really works and helps them move on with their lives and keep a better outlook during often long, drawn-out litigation.

The work of a legal assistant can be stressful at times. Attorneys are, sometimes, difficult to work with and for. They expect a lot out of their staff and expect great self-sufficiency. Most simply don't have time to counsel or train you as well as you'd like. They barely have time to do their own work and/or delegate it to their staff.

Attorneys are also people, mostly very nice people, and can be very generous, interesting, and fulfilling to know.

Work as if it is your own business. By that, I mean, ask yourself, "What should I do with this document or letter? What would I do if the decision were mine to make?" Of course, you must work under the supervision of an attorney, but that state of mind, and the initiative and self-sufficiency it breeds, is what will keep you a step above.

You will learn a lot about life and common sense. You will see trends up front and personal, sometimes even before its hits the mainstream media.

Countless times I have seen newscasts and newspaper articles about say, consumer debts and a rise in personal bankruptcies. But for months before, our firm had a substantial rise in bankruptcy clients drowning in debt…usually credit card debt. This is the type of work that can teach you a "life lesson," maybe a lesson to curb your own credit card spending, take a deeper look at your own finances or make sure your emergency fund is up to par.

Lawyers and their staff, especially legal assistants, sometimes fall into the role of being a counselor. You will need the ability to listen well to people and their stories, to sympathize, even if their predicament was entirely their own doing, and bring to the client comfort, confidence and professionalism.

Tell the client what is going on in their case. Take them, step by step through the process. If they feel a part of it, they will be more at-ease and will be happier clients. Actually explain what is meant by service of process, and other technical terms of which they know nothing, such as, "Your complaint has been filed and we have given the summons to the sheriff or process server and they have to personally serve it upon the Defendant. Once we receive word back from them, I will let you know and we can then proceed." Tell them deadlines, etc. Make sure you adhere to what you are telling them, too. If something gets off track, inform the client and tell them why. People are, as a general rule, extremely understanding if shown the proper respect.

But there is a fine line. Be wary of telling clients too-specific details. And make sure you know what you are talking about when it comes to time frames. People hear what they want to hear and you don't want to get into the habit of telling people, "Your case will be settled in 2 weeks!" when you know it won't, just to get them off the phone. Believe me, those people will be on the phone to you again in *exactly* two weeks demanding answers as to why their case is not settled when you told them it would be. Also, I learned, try to let the attorney exclusively handle money matters. Meaning, if a client asks you how much a case is worth, even in your attorney permits you to discuss these matters with them, be cautious to the extreme of stating that only your boss can discuss those issues with them. Many clients hear, "We have demanded $250,000.00 in your demand letter," and get supremely upset when we urge them to settle for $15,000. They think, "Why has my attorney backed down so much?" Your attorney, or you if that is who the task falls to, must, from the beginning, explain what you are demanding and why. Explain that you always demand *much, much more* than the case is really worth. Then, discuss the true value of the case with them. Discuss the weaknesses in the case— and the ramifications of losing the case. My boss used to say we have to "bring them back to earth." An informed client is usually a happy and *realistic* client. Again, be mindful of not giving any legal advice, simply state, "The attorney asked me to relay to you the Defendant's offer of $7,500." If they ask what you think and should they, "Take the money," as a paralegal, you may not advise them of such things. This could possibly be construed as practicing law without a license, and can get you, your attorney and your law firm into trouble. This is why it is best to have the attorney deal with money issues.

I had a boss who was notorious for telling clients, "We should receive the Defendant's answers to interrogatories within two weeks," after having only mailed them two days ago or, "Your deposition *will* be scheduled within a week."

Now, anyone who has worked in a law firm, especially in a litigation practice, knows that you can make no such promises. In scheduling, you are at the mercy of your own firm's calendar, at least one other attorney's calendar (the opposing counsel), and probably a court reporter's or judge's calendar. I have never told any client that their deposition *will* be scheduled in a certain amount of time. I can give rough estimates, but I am mindful to tell the clients that it is just an estimate and no guarantees. And I give *reasonable* estimates. That same boss used to tell clients he would get a trial date for them in two or three months—right after the case was filed! Now, I don't know what judicial system he was practicing in or even what planet he was on, but unless there is a dire emergency (i.e., a plaintiff or defendant is terminally ill and dying), you simply cannot, and should not, get a trial date two or three months after filing a law suit. That is not enough time to prepare and obtain discovery, take depositions and basically, be ready.

Clients will appreciate your honesty, time and effort to educate them and they will feel like they are a part of their own case. They will feel more in control and comfortable and less nervous. Remember—knowledge is power. Using this approach will also cut down on the calls from clients asking, "What's happening on my case?" You can tell them that it will be at least another thirty more days until you receive and review the other side's discovery responses (not two weeks!) or we will try set some depositions in the next 60-90 days. Keep in touch. Clients truly appreciate these little considerations.

The number one complaint lawyers—and Bar Associations—hear is that lawyers and their offices never call them back and never tell them the status of their case. Just a few minutes on the phone, or even in person with their file right in front of you, will go a long way towards fostering and maintaining a good client relationship. It will conserve time later from trying to "save" a client or calm an irate one down.

Speaking of irate, you will unfortunately encounter people who are just plain rude or inconsolable. Deal with them as best you can, but don't take any cursing or berating. People can be in the worst situations when they call an attorney and try, as a paralegal on the front lines, to react with a bit of patience and willingness to help when they call collect from jail or are going through a divorce and want to vent or are seriously injured. But if these persons become abusive, you have every right tell them to call back when they can be civil, and hang up. Tell the attorney of the client's conduct and he or she will usually see to it that you are not treated that way again.

Finally, some closing insights on the actual work you will be doing as a paralegal.

Prioritization is a key. Knowing what has to be done, what should be done, and what can wait is crucial to your workflow.

Preparing and responding to discovery is interesting, because it seems to pull the whole case together. This is true on both civil and criminal cases. You can organize and focus in on the facts, the witnesses, the client's or other party's background, and the production of documents and exhibits. The pieces to your puzzle's story will be pulled together and completed. But plan your time well because discovery is one of the most daunting and time consuming tasks a legal assistant will encounter. Some larger firms have paralegals working on discovery exclusively.

Other miscellaneous matters would be to obtain prior medical records, obtain social security records, tax records, deal with correspondence between either side, keep track of settlement negotiations, and assist in keeping files organized. Keeping an eye on the small details and the big picture should be a mantra to you, as a legal assistant.

Once all discovery, depositions, motions, and amassing pertinent information is done, on most every case, the case is usually mediated, or may go through another form of alternate dispute resolution. Most of the time, the cases settle at this point. Then the case is over, with no necessity of going to trial!

But for those that don't settle, there is a lot of work ahead (more on that later).

Going to trial is very interesting and educational. I greatly enjoy it.

I get to see exactly how my work is used and what exhibits and witnesses were utilized and how it all plays out in real time. I also love the drama. It's not exactly like television or the movies, but there still is the element of "the gamble" or the "roll of the dice" involved, with the unpredictable variables of a judge and jury.

Juries, I have found, take their jobs very seriously, and from what I have seen, generally make right and fair decisions most of the time. Judges, by and large, are pretty even-handed also, with some obvious and notable exceptions. The lawyers are, despite stereotypic negative public perception, very professional, ethical, and moral, and are simply doing their job to the best of their training and ability, protecting their respective clients' interests.

What's that old adage? One can complain and harp about lawyers, calling them sharks, ambulance chasers, and every other name in the book—until they need one!

Again, most everyone in the legal profession is professional and competent and are just people who are in the midst of a very difficult and stressful field. Imagine your own problems for a moment. Then, multiply those problems by 100 or more. You will then understand what a lawyer's and legal assistant's job is: worrying about and dealing with hundreds or even several hundreds of people's problems.

## GOING, GOING, SETTLE!

Of course, you will find in this day and age, with most jurisdictions requiring some form of mediation prior to trial, and the immensity of some jury verdict awards, that most cases really do settle without ever going before a jury. Which begs the question that I have asked myself and countless others have complained about—how do you stay motivated and work to prepare so hard for trial when you know it seems to be a huge waste of time, because the case is going to settle anyway?

Let's say you have a big case and you are making numerous copies of all exhibits, making blow-ups of crucial exhibits, setting a million depositions for use at trial, getting the whole department working on various tasks and generally going full steam ahead, when….STOP!

The case settled.

Whew!

At first, you celebrate.

"Dodged a bullet!" we all say laughingly.

"We won!" (It's oftentimes thought of as *both* sides winning with a settlement.) And we all plan on leaving early for happy hour at the local pub near the courthouse where we are sure to run into some of the local legal community to gloat about our windfall (without revealing anything confidential, of course).

But when this happens *all the time,* you start thinking, second-guessing. Isn't all this prepping a colossal waste of time? Why bother? How do you get over this feeling that what you are doing is worthless, and stay motivated to do it all over again with the next case, when that one will, by all probability, settle as well?

Well, it is difficult at times, I must say. Sometimes you just know the case will settle out—if liability is unquestioned, if the insurance company seems willing to cough up policy limits, if the tortfeasor was drunk and we can prove it, all of these situations can from the intake phase signal a high likelihood of settlement. The attorneys may be close in monetary numbers, or deals, and you know that the tasks you are doing are just a "show" for everyone involved.

But you have to do them.

Because the one time you don't, the one time you're not fully prepared, you will wind up in front of a judge and jury.

So, we know that the simple answer is that you have to keep going no matter what.

But how to stay motivated?

Well, I like to look at this problem thus:

Even if I am standing at the copy machine for two hours copying needlessly, and making tons of phone calls to coordinate depositions that I will ultimately have to backtrack on and cancel, I think that these things, and many others that I and countless other legal assistants do, *do* help in settling cases, and in many cases can actually help in settling cases, as we show the other side that we are ultimately prepared to go the distance and try the case. It makes the other parties know you're serious. You are prepared, just in case, and adding to your skill and mastery of legal assisting.

I try not to think of it as a waste of time. I try to envision it as, if it helps the case get resolved, then my efforts were not in vain. Also, there really is no choice in the matter, but you can help yourself along with just doing it. You can look at it as a training exercise, or "dress-rehearsal." Next time, you will be more efficient, and trial preparation will take less time, and the few times you actually go to trial, you will be ready, prepared and confident.

That said, I am a HUGE proponent of the process of mediation. I believe it is the one of the best procedures to happen to, or be forced upon, the legal profession—ever. I have seen countless cases settle at mediations, both pre-suit and in litigation, and everyone walks away happy, with no need to unnecessarily burden the court and their already congested dockets, and no need to call six or twelve people from their lives, disrupting their day to day existence, with something that can and should have been resolved by the parties themselves.

In time, with experience and worldliness, I viewed any case very simply, almost bluntly; a case is a problem. We have to find a solution to the problem, i.e., monetary compensation, an apology, a criminal behind bars, or something specific such as one sister returning a piece of jewelry that she was supposed to give to another sister after probating their mother's will. I believe in clients taking an active role in the mediation process and them being told their case is a *problem* that is trying to be solved. What do they really want out of it? What, if they could have anything they want (within reason), would be their solution to this problem? These questions and the assessment process gets people thinking about what they really want out of their case and makes them feel more in control over the outcome.

A very large majority of cases settle either pre-suit (before a lawsuit is filed), during the litigation process, or at mediation. But what happens when they don't? Are there reasons? Yes, many.

Sometimes, the parties are simply unreasonable and too far apart with their desires. One doesn't want to pay, or go to jail, or pay their child support. Sometimes, it's a matter of pride or principle, or simply wanting a day in court or to get back at someone or something. This is true especially in divorce cases—spouses sometimes just want to see their estranged "ex" suffer.

Sometimes, it's the lawyers themselves. It used to irk me when attorneys posture, micro-strategize and basically let pride get in the way of settling a case, and put their own egos and interests above the interests of the client. I have seen cases where the Plaintiff's demand is $75,000, and the Defendant's offer is $72,500, and it *didn't* settle! Geez! Wouldn't anyone try to settle this? I mean, it's soooo close! Lawyers try to bully their clients into not "giving in" or not "paying their top demand." Some lawyers don't get along with each other and it becomes personal (a big ethics violation, but a reality just the same). While I haven't seen this behavior a whole lot, thank goodness, it always saddened me. And, while I do respect the fact that everyone, including lawyers, has their own personal style and stratagem, I do think that looking out for anyone other than a client is just dishonorable, and tarnishes the morality and public opinion of the practice of law.

To prepare a case when it is ready, or scheduled, for mediation (or arbitration, which is another alternative dispute method), you, as a paralegal, should make sure the attorney is prepared by checking to see if all discovery is completed, including all documents received from production, and that the file is organized and in order. In a large majority of cases, especially personal injury litigation, a mediation summary is prepared outlining the issues of a case, facts, including description of the incident, listing of medical expenses and/or wages lost or incurred by the client, perhaps a summary of medical records, and a list of costs incurred by the law firm. Some firms use a form for this where you simply "plug in" the information. If they don't, perhaps you can create one on your own and for others in your firm who may need a "starting point." Below is a checklist that may be helpful to start with and tailor for your own purposes.

Some firms use notebook binders to organize, index and tab documents such as the accident report, all medical records and bills, health insurance information, deposition summaries, case law on certain issues that came up in the case, pertinent pleadings, discovery responses and notes on how the attorney has assessed the case, i.e., how much he or she thinks it is worth, the other side's last proposal of settlement or monetary offer, and the like.

Still other firms use a "video settlement demand" wherein software programs are utilized to bring a document up on the screen which can then be used to highlight egregious, damaging or useful documents, a witness' statement or other integral pieces of the proverbial puzzle. For example, in a nursing home negligence case, an attorney trying to prove fraud, shoddy management and horrible treatment of a resident, may want to highlight the fact that treatment was disclosed by the nursing home as having taken place on, "February 30, 2001 to Ms. Jane Doe." February 30th? There is obviously no such date, which the attorney would then likely use to discredit the nursing home's other documentary production. Or, he or she can bring up a document and use the computer to highlight improper nutrition, or lack of turning and positioning when a doctor has clearly ordered it.

Following you will find the mediation checklist referenced above:

## MEDIATION CHECKLIST

Depending on the case, this list will give you a starting point to begin preparing for a mediation or arbitration:

Personal Injury or Civil Litigation

- Accident or Incident Reports

- Any Contracts between parties, or other pertinent documentation such as receipts, good faith estimates, etc.

- Witness Statements

- Insurance Information (this could include health, homeowners, life, disability, and/or the other parties' insurance information)

- Medical Records

- Medical Bills

- Wage Loss information

- Costs (for your own firm; i.e., how much the law firm has spent so far on this particular matter, which is recoverable out of any settlement)

- Pertinent Pleadings: Complaint, Answers, Discovery Responses, witness and exhibit lists, and any mediation summaries of any other party. Also, any important motions such as motions to dismiss, motions for summary judgment, and motions in limine.

- Case Law and list of issues

- Attorney Notes

Family Law Litigation

- Financial Affidavits and all financial documentation

- Petitions, Answers and Discovery Responses

- Witness Statements

- Costs (if applicable)

- Pertinent Pleadings: Complaint, Answers, Discovery Responses, witness and exhibit lists and any mediation summaries of any other party. Also, any important motions such as motions to dismiss, motions for summary judgment, and motions in limine.

- Case Law and list of issues

- Attorney Notes

## *IN TRIAL*

"In trial" in reality, starts way before a trial ever starts and means lots of planning ahead and building in time for emergencies.

If you are "in trial" with your attorney, actually in the courthouse during a trial, be prepared to sit for long periods of time, take notes on the jury, testimony, and pay close attention to details—oh, and often, try not to fall asleep. Some of the testimony, especially very technical expert testimony, can unremarkably drone on and on.

Know the courthouse, or get to know it, quickly, because if your attorney needs a quick copy of an exhibit for the judge or jury, you will be expected to know where to go to get it done. Know where to park, and for how long before a "boot" is unceremoniously locked to your vehicle. Know the location of the Judicial Assistant (the judge's assistant or secretary). Know restaurants and break rooms and restrooms. Know where your attorney can go with the client to talk privately. All these things, and more, may be crucial. The attorney simply doesn't have time for these little things, but as a legal assistant, you do and you should.

In the courtroom, legal assistants, for the most part, stay behind the bar, that is, they must physically stay behind the bar of the courtroom, which is in actuality a small wooden barrier, usually with a swinging gate or half-door, where the attorneys, jurors, parties, bailiff, clerk of court, and judge sit or stand. Sometimes, judges will allow legal assistants to sit with the attorney at the plaintiff's or defendant's table, but always check in with a particular judge before doing so. You never want to give the impression that you are holding yourself out to be an attorney if you are not, which is unethical, and can reflect poorly on your attorney, who will need every ounce of respect from the judge that he or she can get.

A few weeks prior to a trial of a case, take care of the little things that could be catastrophic if waited for until the last minute, such as making sure you have backup toner for your printers, copiers, and other equipment, and have the supplies you and your attorney will need. A little thought a few weeks prior goes a long way. Even if you are not responsible directly for these things, contact the supplies manager or office manager to ascertain what is on hand and what you think is needed.

Of course, you may know your local courthouse, but what if you are in another jurisdiction, and not familiar with your surroundings? Your resourcefulness, independence and pure grit should then kick in. I recall going from floor to floor in a courthouse that I really didn't know at all, looking for a place to get an extra copy of a document made, an exhibit for the jury, if I recall correctly. I knew that the whole courtroom and the trial was suspended waiting for me to make *one* copy. Well, office to office, floor to floor, smiling sweetly and inquiring as to the location of a copy machine, I finally found someone who could help me and got the copy made. The lesson learned? Keep at it. I have never, to this day, been faced with a task that I could not, eventually, carry out. Another obvious lesson may be to make extra copies of exhibits! But seriously, we do that anyway, and it always seems that there is just *one more* copy that we need during trial. When all else fails, ask the information desk for a map, or see the court administrator's office for assistance—they will usually be glad to point you in the right direction.

Be prepared to run, and I do mean run, to pick up exhibits, witnesses and other details. Fill your gas tank and your purse with quarters for parking downtown, but make sure you save receipts for the attorney or firm to reimburse you, as those are client costs. Tell your spouse you'll be late, if he or she is used to a particular routine or expects you home at a certain time. Carry a cell phone, but know that some courthouses, mainly federal, don't allow cell phones, or any other devices with batteries, unless permitted by a Federal Judge, and turn them off or on silent where appropriate. Arrange back-up babysitting for your kids, or arrange for your spouse or a family member to pick them up at daycare. Expect the unexpected and often chaotic—I can vividly recall preparing additional jury instructions at 11:45 at night on the third day of trial, from home, with the attorney dictating to me over the phone.

To prepare for trial, there is a lot of work to do and the best thing to do is prepare as far ahead as possible, I suggest several weeks, and to utilize a trial checklist tailored to your area of law and your attorney's desires. I have prepared one below as a starting point for you. Your checklist can include such tasks as: depositions to schedule and obtain the transcripts to file with the court, all documents copied for exhibits, have a handle on each sides' witnesses and exhibits, subpoenaing and coordinating witness's testimony, motions in limine, which ask the court to keep something out of the testimony, be it a picture, a reference to an insurance company, or otherwise, and a list of any other pending issues to be addressed prior to a jury being sworn in. Trial prep can include anything from placing stickers on exhibits, marking them properly, to making sure all discovery to be used is actually filed with the court, to preparing a trial notebook for your attorney, to contacting your witnesses to go over with them and familiarize them with their anticipated testimony. Another good rule of thumb would be to obtain and analyze jury verdicts for your particular issue or fact scenario through the Jury Verdict Reporter, or similar types of publications through your local or state bar association. Jury verdict reporters allow you to look at a particular cause of action, for example, trauma-induced fibromyalgia, and see what juries in your area have awarded, if anything, to plaintiffs who have taken such matters to trial. This can allow your attorney to better assess the case, its relative attractiveness to juries in the area, and construe the risks of going to trial.

Presenting evidence is also a way that paralegals may become intimately involved in the trial of a case. Like an archeologist digging through sedimentary and volcanic ash layers for fossil assemblages and attempting to date them accurately in the geologic time scale, attorneys and their paralegals have to sift through many layers of time, testimony, documents and witness accounts and place them into understandable and logical context, so that a jury can easily comprehend all of what they are seeing and draw the same or similar conclusions as your attorney is arguing to them. They must interpret the evidence and piece together the "era" or timeline of a case's facts, and base a decision upon same.

For example, how do you portray invasive medical treatments for a medical malpractice case in order to have maximum impact upon the jury? How do you depict or demonstrate the number of rehab visits or the number of home health care treatments, or illustrate for the jury how debilitating and demoralizing it was for the Plaintiff to lose her hair from rehabilitative chemical therapy brought on by a doctor's misdiagnosis? How may the jury be educated about a crime scene, or make simple sense out of the massive amount of financial documents of a wife hiding or secreting monies and investments from her soon-to-be ex-husband (in an unrelated civil matter, not the divorce itself, which does not go to a jury)?

Having had to deal with these and many other similar states of affairs, I like to use chronological timelines, charts, graphs and other visual clues to tie together the, sometimes, thinly entwined rope of facts, opinions, evidence, and witness testimonies. Remember when preparing that we are all kids at heart—we all want to see pretty, colorful pictures, and the easier and more visual you can make it for a jury, the more likely they are to tie in the visual information with the arguments and position of your attorney. These methods work especially well in cases where there are overwhelming amounts of records, witness testimony, and expert opinions or where the case is very technical or complex. The ability to unravel the rope of knotted information for the jury or judge will render you, your attorney, your client, and everyone involved, organized, efficient, and sharp.

Here are a few real-life examples upon which I have honed my skills.

During a huge case involving a low-impact motor vehicle accident with a client with numerous pre-existing back problems, we wanted, and needed, to show the jury the "explosion" in treatment for his back problems from prior to the accident and subsequent to the occasion. But how to do this, in as effective a manner as possible?

First, we tirelessly sifted through all medical records from both before and after the date of the accident. We tabbed and clearly labeled every single reference to back pain. Then, we added up the number of visits and treatments for back pain before and after the unfortunate event. We then created a simple pie graph showing that the number of back pain visits before the accident was 17, while the number of visits for back pain after the accident was 147! This could plainly and clearly show the jury the upsurge of times that this person sought treatment after the accident, furthering the case that the accident exacerbated the pre-existing condition.

Likewise, for another injury matter, we created a calendar chart wherein we painstakingly and with great consumption of time thumbed through literal stacks of records, making a list of all therapy visits, doctor visits, pain injection procedures and hospitalizations. We then color coded these events, such as all therapy visits being color blocked in blue, all hospitalizations in green, etc. We then gave this information to our exhibit vendor where they shaded in each appropriate box, each of which represented a day on the calendar, for the particular event. For example, if March 4-8, 2000, was a hospitalization, those days were shaded in green. When completed, the jury could visually see the amount of "greens" or hospitalizations over a few year period, the number of "blues" spent in therapy, the amount of time spent in doctors offices, and the total number of days this poor soul spent in agony after a treatment.

These visual aids can make events and facts understandable to a jury, and can create a sense out of the mountains of information on a case, especially technical or very complex medical matters.

As a paralegal doing trial work, knowing of and using a good legal exhibit vendor can be an extremely positive tool in trial presentation technique. Having done exhibit work for many firms, they usually have tons of original and creative ideas on how to present cases, and have templates for diagrams, accident reconstruction, timelines, charts, graphs, and other ideas to use at trial. These days, many legal exhibits are being computerized and are being shown on a big screen in the courtroom via a computer monitor projector. This can be expensive, but I believe this is a growing trend that is going to be seen more and more in the future. Courthouses are growing ever more "hooked up," as well, with most courtrooms having internet access or CAT5 cable ready wiring or outlets, so that attorneys and parties can use laptops if the court permits.

Mistrials, which are generally where a Judge declares that the trial cannot continue for some legal error or dysfunction of the procedure, are always in the back of attorneys' minds and do occur more often than one might think. Mistrials happen for a variety of reasons—some completely out of anyone's control. On that fateful, heartbreaking day, September 11, 2001, I was physically in a courtroom during opening arguments of a personal injury car accident trial. Of course, due to the unfolding tragic events, I quickly hovered around the television in the judicial assistant's office with the rest of the judicial staff. But as time wore on, and the day grew more horrific, the judge declared a mistrial and we eventually evacuated the courthouse.

Other reasons for mistrials run the gamut from a plaintiff suffering a nervous breakdown, to an attorney suffering a sudden death in their family, or a witness, attorney or party uttering a totally inappropriate or improper statement on the stand, in front of the jury, assuring a mistrial. Then, although you as a paralegal may get a temporary reprieve from trial intensity, a mistrial just means you likely will have to prepare to try the case all over again—another day and another time.

Being in trial also means lending moral support to your boss. Offer to and listen to his or her opening statement, closing remarks, direct and cross examinations, voir dire of potential jurors, and your client's testimony. Always be truthful—your opinion is valued, and the attorney needs the unadulterated version, not a vague opinion. Just be tactful. Attorneys have feelings too. You can think that the case is somewhat less than credible or even that the jury will slam your client and he'll lose big-time. But try to focus on specifics, such as, telling the attorney that you feel that the client comes across abrasively and you are afraid this will alienate the jury, or being concerned with two of the medical records that have major discrepancies between what they state and what the client says happened. Likewise, pointing out and highlighting key and high points can also be helpful.

Attorneys often get pumped up—somewhat like girding for battle, strapping on greaves of armor, a sword, a bow, actual warfare, with strategizing, sizing up the "enemy" (opposing party), and contingency plans for events that may go awry. A good number of attorneys refer to their conference rooms where they spread out a case and prepare for trial, their "war rooms." Some firms have "battle cries" they chant down the hallway before going to trial:

*Going to battle, going to trial,*
*won't see me for a while*
*When I get back, you will see,*
*I'll have a great big win for me!*

Some lawyers hang flags. I know one firm who hangs a white flag outside the respective attorney's office if they lose and a pirate flag if they win. Some use stuffed animals. For instance, we used to, somewhat teasingly, call one of my bosses, "A tiger in the courtroom." Subsequently, we bought a stuffed tiger in a cage and "let it out" whenever a big case was coming up. Music can also be a big booster for motivating the "general and the troops". Your attorney may relax to the velvety Barry Manilow or soulful Mariah Carey, the heart blasting metal groove of Slipknot, or the crusade cries and sentiment of Creed. Maybe even R&B, rap, gospel music or motivational tapes— whatever works to get him or her motivated! It may seem like fun and games for such serious business, but these little traditions and rituals are both needed, helping to cope with stress, and comforting to all involved in the preparation for something so huge and taxing. Whatever it takes to get you and your boss propelled into your trial mode, within reason and norms of good taste, go ahead and try. It is almost like studying for a comprehensive, closed-book, all essay final exam where you have to know a whole slew of facts, statistics and information off the top of your head, at the drop of a pin.

Because this is it.

The trial is your last real chance to do anything on the case.

It's now or never.

But then there's the appeal! There is a reason that there are appellate attorneys—it is a highly specialized area of practice and presents its own rules, problems, deadlines, and idiosyncrasies. A good portion of cases, even if your side wins, will lag due to the other side exercising their right to appeal, and doing so based on a claimed error they assert was made during the trial, or before, that worked a substantial hardship upon their client, a new trial, or some other reversal of a trial court's action. This process could take months, if not years from the original date of the verdict. Typically, very proficient writers and "paper-arguers" become appellate lawyers. We typically outsourced our appeals work, meaning, we used to turn an appeal over to an attorney who specifically did appeals and let him handle the case from then on.

For appeals, you must know the timelines, which are extremely strict and draconian, and how to argue a case on paper, for the most part, as the court sometimes and often does not permit oral arguments. You must also know the very exacting format that courts require for appeals such as the margins permitted, the exact font and size, the requirements of having a Table of Contents, Table of Authorities (case law), and the maximum number of pages allowed. If you are a paralegal working on appeals, you will probably be researching, analyzing the record on appeal (everything on record such as exhibits, testimony, etc.), keeping track of deadlines and perhaps drafting all or portions of the actual briefs to be submitted to the court to argue your position.

## TRIAL CHECKLIST

- Schedule all depositions and obtain all transcripts to file with the court

- Make sure everything your attorney needs admitted as evidence actually gets filed with the court. (In most jurisdictions, actual discovery responses, i.e., interrogatory answers and responsive documents, are not initially filed with the court.)

- Schedule any last minute witness interviews or expert witness meetings to go over testimony prior to trial

- Make sure you have all discovery responses as well as non-party production responses

- Blow up or have prepared, exhibits to use at trial and place appropriate exhibit stickers or markers on them (depending on the jurisdiction)

- Subpoena and coordinate witness's testimony

- Prepare and file any motions in limine (which ask the court to keep something out of the testimony, be it a picture, a reference to an insurance company, or otherwise, and a list of any other pending issues to be addressed prior to a jury being sworn in)

- Prepare a trial notebook with all pertinent pleadings, discovery responses, motions, witness and exhibit lists, attorney notes, depositions and witness statements, and case law.

- Obtain and analyze jury verdicts for your particular issue or fact scenario through the Jury Verdict Reporter or other such publications.

- Contact the court for any special needs, i.e., time for pre-trial hearings, translators, courtroom equipment, scheduling difficulties of witnesses, etc.

- Confirm with your client; judge, court reporter and witnesses

- Make sure all documents are copied (usually 3 copies – one for your attorney, one for the other attorney, and one (usually the originals) for the court or judge to submit as evidence)

- Double check other parties' witnesses and exhibits, and make sure your attorney meets with the other side to go over exhibits or otherwise knows exactly what the other side is planning to introduce

- Organize the file in a logical fashion so that the attorney can find anything and everything quickly and easily

- It is also a good idea to create a "supply drawer" for your attorney to take to trial. What I did was take an expandable file folder, (but I have also used plastic containers and boxes) and throw in a stapler, staples, staple remover, rubber bands, paper clips, binder clips, pens, pencils, markers, highlighters, pads, sticky notes, and anything else I think he may need, such as extra tabs for his or her trial notebook. Believe me, you absolutely <u>need</u> these supplies with you at trial and the attorney may not have time to think about this small, but significant task!

# *BURNOUT*

A few words about burnout and balance:

I recall the trip of a lifetime my parents took my sister and I on when we were 13 years old. We went on a month-long trip to the Grand Canyon, and most of the western National Parks, winding up in the tundra of Glacier National Park, and finally, flying home to sunny Florida from rainy Seattle, Washington. What a journey it was! During that trip, we went white-water rafting for two days down the Colorado river, rolling through the belly of the river-carved, dazzling Grand Canyon. That expedition filled me, even to this day, with a sense of adventure, exploration, and pioneering. It was the best "in the moment" feeling ever! On the river, with the stratified canyon walls impossibly impressive rising up on either side, you cannot worry about the rapids behind you, or the falls that lay ahead. You must concentrate on the gyrating water you are in *right now*!

This life experience sure was fun at the time, but also gave me something to keep with me forever—the knowledge that I can chart the best course of action with the information I have, follow through with that plan, and if *not* all goes well, overcome obstacles and move on to the next set of blockages, and the next and the next.

Being a legal assistant is a wonderful career, but it can sometimes be extremely stressful, with a sky-scraping workload, vast and immense responsibilities, and, in working for some attorneys and people, dealing with mammoth egos and thorny personalities.

I remember being extremely excited, giddily so, as I began my first class in the paralegal program I attended at our local community college. I devoured the books, the subject matter, the legal, Latin words and the whole concept of law and its practice.

This was the first stepping stone to my new career!

I stuck with the program, through Business Law, Contracts, Family Law, Real Estate, Litigation and Ethics. Finally, after what seemed like years, and actually was, I graduated! As I stood on the steps of the convention center, in my blue cap and gown, with my family around me, I felt I was on the right path and had found a good, solid career. I also took the CLA exam shortly thereafter, passed it and sucked into my soul everything to do with the field of legal assisting. I just knew I would be making a difference in the legal profession!

Over twelve years later, I believe I have done just that.

But over the course of my career, especially after leaving my personal injury law firm job after five years, and again, working double time at my full-time job and at my husband's firm, severe burnout set in, which peaked and ebbed like a bell curve, or a perpetual tsunami. During the ascent to the top of the curve of being burned out, my spirit imploded, sparking a supernova of mixed emotions and frustrations.

I have gone through a couple of periods when I couldn't seem to find my "fire," my drive, anymore. During these years, I felt like I could not get motivated. I was cynical, jaded, and skeptical about the clients, the lawsuits, and lawyers in general. I thought distortion of facts and posturing were rampant. I felt most of the work I did all day long was useless and just went to help people who didn't deserve to be helped. Of course, this was not true, except for a few cases, but it felt like negativity and pointlessness had encircled my galaxy of work, demeaning all I had striven to accomplish over the years, and had erupted into a red giant, about to incinerate my career and myself.

Before that happened though, I would have to finally realize that, as a paralegal I was not going to change the entire world—but I could change how I saw it and dealt with it, and I could certainly make a difference is some clients' lives. To do this, I looked back.

I recalled the excitement of walking into a cool, well-appointed law office from the searing Florida sun and knowing I was up for anything anyone threw at me. I was actually excited to be standing at a copy machine making copies! Fax something? No problem. I was part of a team who made cases stronger, better, and made people's problems *and* their cases, easier to resolve. What could be better?

I lured back my remembrances of my first job where I filed papers like no other, with the dedication of a librarian in the Smithsonian Institute's Library. I remember setting goals every day. File faster, better, more efficiently.

Throughout my career, as the attorneys gave me more work, I myself realized I could do better and better, become more efficient, more productive, more profitable for the firms. I finally realized that I could not only do better, I could handle anything. I tried to focus on that mind set whenever my career came across this transform boundary of going back and forth between liking and detesting my choice of career.

As my career progressed, and the cycles of burnout and content came and went, I learned from these rotations and realized that most everyone has them! The trick is getting back on the proper track and achieving balance. As I became more experienced in my career and with the wisdom of workplace hardship and coping skills, I became much more confident in my personal life also, and began to explore other hobbies and interests.

The happiest legal assistants I know are those with a life outside of the office. They take a painting or pottery class. They walk three times a week. They volunteer for their son's Boy Scout troop. They coach and cheer on their daughter's soccer team. Compete in triathlons. Read a book a week.

I went through ruts just like everyone, when all you seem to do is work, go home, sleep, work, go home, sleep…it seems like a vicious cycle. I dreaded going to work sometimes and didn't think I could stand one more day of talking to clients, typing documents and working with difficult attorneys.

Then, after a while, I remembered that I would have to use self-realization and introspection to change my attitude. Actually, I altered more than just my attitude, I cleared the way to a new lifestyle. As before, *I* was the one who changed. I knew deep down that I wanted to stay in the legal assisting field, I just had to learn to deal with it, with the varied stresses and personalities, better. A new job in a new environment would have meant, for me, substituting the same thing. Is the grass necessarily always greener? Not always.

So, after my last cycle of this seeming despair, I signed up for writing classes, which have been on the back burner in my life for years. I competed in my first 5K race (I proudly brought up the rear thank you very much!). I worked on scrapbooking, a new favorite hobby of mine, which I do with my sister and a group of close personal friends, making permanent memories for my family to enjoy for decades to come. I read more books, something in which I have found solace my entire life. I spent more time with my family, friends, and husband. And I somehow, slowly, through the morass of chaos and adversity, achieved a contented balance.

Even in the every day life at the office, I gained a new equilibrium. I took mental stretches or "brain breaks." For instance, if I just finished three hours of discovery work, without getting up from my chair at all, I wrapped my work up, and logged on to the internet for a moment to check the news or something fun like my online horoscope. It's just for a few minutes and certainly everyone needs to mentally take a stretch, just like their physical bodies must. Of course, be mindful if your workplace prohibits this kind of personal web-browsing. Other cerebral time outs, such as stepping outside, getting a snack or drink or walking down the hall for a few minutes gives you time to refresh yourself and gear up for the work ahead.

Balance.

That is the ultimate goal in this seesaw of life. Looking forward to something outside of work will help you achieve your own balance and fizzle any burnout threatening to creep in. And, like one hand helping the other, your work life will, in turn, balance your outside life.

# CHAPTER IV

# THE PEOPLE

My husband has an amazing ability. You can almost see problems rolling off of his back—it's as if he has an on/off switch that he can manipulate to deal with stress. What matters to him, he puts his effort into full bore. What does not matter to him, stress, worry, hardship, destructive things, he simply ignores and does not let affect him.

Me, you can practically view hurtful feelings from a petty remark seeping into my cells and stay there, steaming, for days. I am a very sensitive person and take things personally. In the legal field, this is terrible. I learned that being thin-skinned is one of the worst traits to have. Unfortunately, this is a trait which I strongly possess.

If someone said to me, even nicely, that I had made a mistake, or if I found out myself that I screwed up, I would just melt. I get so upset at myself and think I have to be 100% perfect all the time that it would affect me for days. I would double and triple check myself, and proofread simple things such as notes to the file, to the extent of compulsively reading the notes I had added to a file ten times, before I would be satisfied. What was wrong with me?

Obsessive? No. Well maybe a little.

Perfectionist? Yes.

Higher-than-can-be-expected standards? Absolutely. I am an idealist through and through.

Eventually, although it took over a decade, I have discovered to simply learn from my mistakes, try to identify how I made the mistake, and continue on. Oh sure, I would still be upset at myself, but had come to realize than nobody is perfect, not me or anyone else, and that this is just a fact of life. I took a lesson from professional athletes and "parked" my mistakes. Mentally, I would walk in a beautiful garden, and stop to sit on a bench to "park" my problem. I would think about it, then get up and leave it behind on the bench. This was a good exercise to try to alleviate my fanatical worrying about things that could no longer be changed.

I also realized (again, after almost a decade) that if I, personally, was satisfied with my work product, then I am content that I put forth 100% and tried my best. Even when an attorney, client, or other person is unsatisfied with the work, or if there is someone you simply can't please, I am still fine with my self and my work product, because I know I did the best I possibly could, as I was trained to do in school and over a decade of working in law firms in various areas of law. This is a vital mental outlook, to me, as the most important person you will encounter and rely on in the paralegal field is yourself!

You will meet a lot of interesting people in this profession, such as judges, attorneys, clerks, other legal assistants, and experts in a wide array of fields. Often, you also deal with other community professionals such as doctors, accountants, and engineers.

Some of my legal assistant friends and I have sort of an aphorism about the different backgrounds and personalities of the characters of our field—they are a daily lesson in psychology along with a double scoop of humor.

Once, when I first began working as a paralegal, I was a bit intimidated speaking with a gentleman who was to be our expert witness in a case, who seemed to have a Ph.D. in *everything* and whose Curriculum Vitae was a novella unto itself. I have always greatly admired academic types who are worldly, well-rounded, adventurous, and curious about life and seemed to know the meaning, purpose, and inner workings of just about everything. Those types bring to mind persons such as Carl Sagan, the astronomer and science popularizer, and members of the famed Leakey family with their hugely seminal hominid and early-human archaeological finds. In other words, these were people who knew what they wanted, went after it, kept at it, achieved it, and eventually achieved it to an extent that others can only dream. But, in time, I learned that the expert witnesses that we used were also just people doing what they do best, through training and life experience.

The age-old adage works here—be nice and you will be treated nicely back. Be respectful and you will most always be respected right back. Build a good rapport with your expert witnesses because, more than likely, you will use them again and again in numerous cases. Also, if you do a certain type of law, like so many firms, you may also deal with a lot of the same opposing counsel, opposing law firms and their staff. Once they get to know you, you will learn which ones are slow to respond, fast in getting back their discovery responses, nice, accommodating, business-like, stressed out, or laid back. This information assists you and will be invaluable if you get to know these nuances of your own little circle of people you regularly deal with.

Judicial Assistants, or judge's secretaries, run the gamut of personalities and aptitudes, as in any profession. But always, always treat them with respect and be pleasant to them, because they can be your best friend if you consistently deal with them pleasantly and professionally. If not, you will, trust me, be on their "List." And not their good list if you know what I mean. They have the ear of the Judge, and if they like you, they can be the difference in that hearing being scheduled next week or two months from now.

Other persons at the courthouse and on the judge's staff could include law clerks, law students such as interns, bailiffs, security personnel, clerks and administrative support. They all have a job to do to keep the cycle of justice well-oiled and running as top-notch as it can. Get to know your local team and you will be immensely valuable to your attorney and your firm. One bailiff at the local courthouse, a grandfatherly, sweet old man, always kept candy in his pocket and passed it out to me every time I was there. He made a point to give candy to all the girls, secretaries, paralegals, runners. He was always encircled with friends and is fondly revered.

Other paralegals can and often will be your greatest resource. They can, if you become friendly with them and become involved in your local and/or state paralegal associations, assist you in climbing the ladder in the legal community. They will keep an eye out for jobs, who is where, who is moving, which firms are breaking up or have broken up, forming, merging, etc.

You may also have an office manager in your realm sooner or later. Years into my profession, I found myself acting as the *de facto* office manager. In addition to keeping track of office supplies and long distance service, I lent a hand in delegating workflow, hiring, and "letting go" of a few substandard paralegals. I learned from almost the *second* someone walked in on the first day, whether they were average, below average, above average, or a true stand-out. How did I know? Well, for one, the stand-outs were more often than not, early. Two, they tended to write everything down, in the manner I have discussed herein. Three, they were cheerful, helpful and eager to jump right in. The average ones showed up on time, but did not write things down, seemed to watch the clock until 5:00 p.m., and made sure they got their coffee first. (Hey I know java is a jump start in the morning, but don't run for it immediately on your first day— remember—first impressions!) The below average persons showed up late, or not at all! And, if they did show up, they certainly didn't write anything down, seemed bored and "put out" by the amount of work, complained about the hectic pace and the amount of work, and generally did not seem enthusiastic about their job. These types are also likely to have stretched the truth on their resumes, sometimes a little, sometimes a lot! From this experience, as long as someone in the firm can act as a teacher, mentor or supervisor, I firmly believe in taking work ethic over experience or education any day as skills can be learned but personal practices are tough to teach. But if I had my pick, the ideal person would have the whole package: great habits, as well as education, and experience. It's the whole package that will make you a great employee, a great co-worker, or a great boss!

Your boss, the lawyer, is your biggest priority. Your job is to make yourself, as well as your attorney and law firm look as professional and efficient as possible. There will be people who will try to steer you their way, rather than towards your real focus of the firm and its clientele. Always keep your priority to your boss, your firm and the clients. I recall an opposing attorney who called me to ask where my perpetually late boss was. He was, of course, running behind for a doctor deposition by his usual 15-20 minutes. I told the opposing counsel that my attorney was on the way and should be there shortly. This opposing attorney proceeded to loudly and rudely *demand* that I call my boss on his cell phone and tell him that if he was not there in the next five minutes, the opposing counsel would terminate the deposition. Well, I had just spoken to my boss on his cell phone and he was in the elevator going up to the deposition and would be there in mere minutes. There was just no way that I was going to permit another attorney, who I don't even work for, to order me around, especially after acting like a jerk. So, I hung up on him, turned back to my desk and proceeded to work, without making a follow-up phone call to my employer. Let the attorneys deal with these things amongst themselves. There is only so much you can do. In this case, I knew my boss just could *not* be on time no matter how hard he tried (in truth, though, he didn't really try). Maybe it was in his genes. Anyway, a paralegal's work can transform into a bit of a babysitting service in looking after some attorneys, but you do have to draw the line somewhere. I mean, if an adult can't be on time after earning all those degrees and after 35 or 40 years, what can you do about it? Nothing! What's that saying? Old dog…new tricks?

Clients are the persons who mean the most to your law firm. Without them, there is no law firm, no need to practice law. Again, there are nice clients and difficult clients. Most people come to a lawyer with a major problem, be it a divorce, grievous personal injury, or a potentially liberty-robbing criminal charge. These people are already stressed, possibly angry, emotionally charged, and are usually not interested in being anywhere near warm and fuzzy. They need help, fast, and they have come to your attorney for answers to their dilemma. They want their fears to be put to rest, or at least identified and explained. I have found that paralegals will usually have a large amount of contact with clients, even more so than attorneys. If you can explain to them briefly what is happening, why and what to expect next, of course without giving actual legal advice, and give them small peace of mind, the clients will come to appreciate, respect and count on you to see them through a difficult time in their lives. This can be a very fulfilling aspect of the legal assisting career. Of course it is difficult not to become impatient and critical of clients sometimes. It is fine if you feel this way, just do your best not to show it, or it might reflect poorly on your lawyer. After all, you are only human, but more importantly, *so are clients*, meaning that at times, you will see them at their worst.

One client whined, complained, cajoled, and made a constant pest of herself. She would call the office every day, sometimes numerous times a day, to talk not about her case, but about the soap operas she was watching, the lack of good news on T.V., and her cat. Not her case, but her cat.

How did I deal with this? Well, back in the cave days before caller ID, I got "caught" by her *a lot*. I was a good listener, and always cordial. I realized she was a lonely woman who really just wanted to talk to someone and feel important. I assured her that her case was moving along, kept her updated on happenings, but also did not allow her to interfere with my time to work. I spoke with her for a moment or so, then I would let her know that I had an important meeting, phone call, etc., to attend to and I would keep her informed of her case as soon as we heard something. Clients are people with their own lives, emotions, opinions and backgrounds. Thanks to the recent prevalence of caller ID, with a client such as the one listed above, I would screen her calls and make sure I called the client back on my own time, when he or she wasn't interfering with the other clients and work to be done.

Clients can also be corporations, sometimes big organizations, often faceless, but equally important, especially to a firm. In these instances, you will likely deal with an agent, representative or contact of the company. Of course, these are people too, but these persons are busier, and usually do not have the time to poke around on the phone, although you may be faced with difficult personalities from this segment of clientele as well. Corporate clients, always conscious of their time and the "bottom line," usually like to be dealt with in as short and sweet manner as possible—they want the information they need, now, and then have other duties to which to attend. I have found that e-mail is a valid and useful tool to keep the corporate client updated and satisfied, and gives them a writing to take back to their superior or board of directors. Keep them informed, respect their time, and you should develop and foster a good working relationship.

This is not to say corporate clients are stuffy and stodgy. I have developed numerous great associations with corporate agents and representatives.

Other people and occupations you may meet, speak to, or become acquainted with or exposed to in the paralegal profession are insurance adjusters, accountants and economists, vocational rehabilitation specialists, mediators, arbitrators, physicians, medical staff, police officers, criminal justice workers, and the television and newspaper media.

No other profession that I know of can give you a free ticket into so many people's "backstages;" into their genuine and diverse wisdom, skills, experiences and lives. Taking away even a tiny piece from each person can help to transform your own soul and essence into a more well-rounded and advanced, fascinating being.

There is one final story about the people you will likely meet and work with that I just have to share.

I have an identical twin sister, also an experienced paralegal, and a wonderful person, who has worked in a big firm in the South for several years. She told me of two legal assistants, ensconced in an inter-office battle, who absolutely despised each other (note: there are usually these types in every office!). Anyway, apparently one day the copy machine proved to be witness to what is now known in local paralegal circles as, "The Great Copy Room Brawl." One legal assistant wanted to use the machine, and was using it at the same time the other came in and also wanted to use the machine. They argued, and fisticuffs were threatened between the two, who already had a reputation for disliking the other. Mayhem ensued, actual punches flew and the senior partner, hearing the commotion, fired them and threw them both out on the spot! They were lucky no criminal mischief charges were brought against them.

Here's a free piece of advice to help you keep your job (and potentially out of jail): don't let *anything*, no matter how egregious, escalate into violence in the workplace! The best thing to do with a person you don't like, even deeply and fundamentally, is to keep your distance. And, as part of your employment, if you must interact with them, be as professional and polite as you can, and, again, *put everything in writing*, no matter how militant this may make you feel or seem. Remember that individuals like this will look for a way to trip you up and belittle you to coworkers or the boss, and that your most important ally is yourself and your good habits.

What's another seed to take away from this story? Plant it in your head that no matter how bad your co-workers may seem, you can bet that there's always worse out there somewhere!

# CHAPTER V

# QUALITIES THAT MAKE AN EXCEPTIONAL LEGAL ASSISTANT AND HOW TO STAND OUT FROM THE REST

As in any profession, and as we have discussed and seen first-hand, there are always going to be good and bad individual workers in the legal assisting field, as in any field of work. There are also those who shine above the rest and inspire others around them. Those persons are leaders and there are certain qualities and habits that they share. Are they born that way? Of course not!

Can you be one of those legal assistants who rise above the pack and achieve greatness? Absolutely you can!

The legal assistants who stand out are easy to spot, but are not necessarily superhuman, nor do they possess any skills or habits that you cannot perfect and use to your advantage. The large number of graduates of legal assisting programs may make competition for the top jobs tighter in the future, but, a confident, well-rounded legal assistant who has the whole package: education, work ethics and experience should always find a place in the legal field.

I had the honor of writing an article on this very subject for *Legal Assistant Today* magazine. My feature appeared in the March/April, 2002, issue. The article delved into most of the same ten qualities here that, I believe, if adhered to and honed, will make you an exceptional legal assistant, co-worker and employee. I have also related some real-life examples of exactly how to implement these qualities into everyday practice. Some of this material also summarizes traits, experiences and happenings already discussed in this book, giving you a place to go for a quick reference or refresher.

# 1. BE RESOURCEFUL

Let's say your attorney has asked you to find an obscure expert for the biggest case in the office, and you still can't find one after scouring your firm's expert files and the yellow pages. You don't want to walk into the attorney's office and admit that you could not find an expert. What do you do?

Stop!

Think about your goal—finding an expert in a particular field of expertise. Then think of how to achieve that goal. There is most often a way; it is your job to find it. Perhaps the internet? Or maybe call your local university or college for a professor who may have contacts in that field. Call a friend or colleague at another law firm who might have a contact. There are also associations and clubs for just about everything. I have even used a consumer group hotline to direct me to an expert who knew a certain area of product liability.

When you do find the perfect expert witness for your case, keep his or her Curriculum Vitae and information such as fees and rates for services, in an expert file folder, file cabinet, or computer file. Chances are, you will need this expert again in the future, and if not, you have a reference or referral to give to someone else who might need a similar expert.

Using your resourcefulness and imagination will lead to impressive solutions to your attorney's most time consuming dilemmas. You want to be identified as the person who knows what to do and how to get it done. If you are that person, you will be invaluable and will become an infinitely sought-after problem-solver.

# 2. BE ORGANIZED

Organization, generally, is a mammoth part of legal assisting, and a quality to sharpen and hone. Being able to efficiently locate and utilize documents, exhibits and the like is a trait that is extremely crucial and important to a law firm.

Some people are naturally organized. But what if you are not? Don't worry. You're not doomed, and can learn this fundamental skill. First, take inventory of what is on your desk. Know exactly what work is in your in-box, and what is expected of you. Use calendars, deadline ticklers, and keep meticulous notes. If you just can't seem to create an organized way of preparing and sorting your work, enlist the help of others. Seek another paralegal who is organized and have him or her help you. I personally served as an "organizing mentor" to a paralegal who wasn't really disorganized, but didn't exactly know how to go about her work and keep prioritized. I did show her my proprietary system and with a little practice, she turned out to be very organized and efficient. And most, importantly, she kept at it, made the system personal to her taste, and continued to improve on it.

Being organized will first and foremost help yourself, both with your workload, and with alleviating some of the natural stresses of the workplace. It will perhaps make your job easier and even seem less overwhelming. Most every firm has a filing system in place, and will expect you to use it. As long as documents and other things are filed in a logical, structured fashion, your work and work life should flow smoothly. Also, when your attorney asks about your last conversation with Mr. Client, you can simply pull out your notes and immediately answer. Or, if he calls in a panic asking for the Mrs. Client deposition transcript and summary, you can go to that file, look for the deposition file, and pull it out—no digging through various piles strewn around the office!

Organization will also help your fellow co-workers, supervisors, and others having a hand in the file. For example, everyone gets sick at least infrequently and most will go on vacation at some point each year. What if you are not physically at work or are unreachable by phone? If you are structured and use your organizational skills, your attorney or co-workers should have no problems locating a file or note, or interpreting what you left behind.

One of my past legal assistant colleagues was an absolute slob. Looking at the pathway to her desk, cluttered and lined with stacks and mounds of documents, I did not even attempt to look for anything that I might need, for fear of knocking over massive piles of paper or disturbing Jimmy Hoffa. There must have been a million pieces of paper on and around her desk and yellow sticky notes on every surface, including the walls, floor, the phone, her computer monitor, and in one notable instance, the ceiling (even I can't explain that one!). Anyway, imagine what a chore it was when ever I had to go find something in her office, no matter how small or big—it was next to impossible. I would simply wait until she got back to the office from vacation or wherever, or make do without. Of course, this resulted in a delay in work getting done. Despite being knowledgeable, this person lacked the outside appearance of being efficient and organized. Our boss confided in me that he could not fully respect her as a worker because of the way she kept herself and her office. It was just messy and sloppy. And the shoddiness even carried over into the way she prepared letters and documents. Let's just say that letters should not start at the extreme top of the page and end with, "If you have any questions, please feel me!" Missing a "free to contact" somewhere? This is a good example of why the attorney should read and review *every* document that leaves the office, because his or her reputation may be riding on it—and yours as well.

Being organized and efficient is vital to surging ahead of the rest of the pack. The legal profession, and legal assisting, is growing by leaps and bounds, and there is much competition; but by creating an orderly, methodical, but universally useful environment, you will command respect from your boss, your colleagues, and support staff. And almost more importantly, your co-workers will sincerely appreciate and respect you whether you are at your desk or lying in bed sick, trekking through the mountains or lying on the beach on your vacation.

## 3. PLAN AHEAD AND PRIORITIZE

Just as in planning your dream rendezvous in Paris or that mountain climb in Nepal down to the last detail; hotel stay, rental car, ski rentals, hiking equipment, activities, or planning a party with multiple hors d'voures, courses, and guests, you must plan your work in order for it to be a success.

How to get started? Take a look first at your calendar and deadlines. Make it a regular practice to look ahead for those deadlines approaching in two or three weeks. Start preparing and working on them right now, because the normal course of business, and the unexpected nature of unanticipated things that arise will make that time proverbially fly by. Also, first thing in the morning, get into the habit of looking at the calendar for the next day's schedule. If there is a hearing, pull the file. Make sure all filing is up to date on that file and make the attorney aware of any "red flags" or important notes on a case, such as a recent call from the client or recent correspondence from the opposing counsel. In short, prepare the attorney for any contingencies he or she needs to know prior to attending the hearing or meeting, so that they are not caught off guard. Your attorney will likely be impressed by your strategic thinking and you will not feel constantly hurried preparing last minute tasks.

My boss used to overly rely on me for all deadlines in the office—hearings, discovery, filing of lawsuits, statutes of limitations, everything. He would not know anything he had to do—he knew that *I knew* and that was enough for him. Shouldering such responsibility is alternately both flattering and extremely burdensome. My boss realized I was a planner to an extreme, not a procrastinator, nor someone who was in a state of denial as to the heavy workload. His reliance on me was justified, as I never did miss any deadline, but it certainly heaped more stress on me.

The lawyer I worked for, on the other hand, was a classic dawdler, procrastinator, lollygagger, general cut-up, and our work habits clashed from time to time. I found that a good majority of attorneys are procrastinators and want to wait until the last minute to do everything. Either that or they simply have too much work for any one human being to possibly do. I have found that most attorneys with this trait have been that way since high school and college, waiting until the evening before to start that fifty-page term paper, or master's thesis. Again, old dogs...new tricks. Legal assistants where I'm from have a saying that their attorney bosses all took and passed "Procrastination 101" in law school—with straight A's!!! Seriously, attorneys seem to wait until the last possible minute to do something they knew they had to do weeks ago! Why?

Procrastinators are either afraid of failing, afraid of winning (and therefore being expected to do something all the time), bad time managers, or they simply do not really want to do a certain something. They often simply deny the workload and don't do it, until the deadline is looming like a vicious cloud about to unleash its hurricane-force driving rain and winds. Attorneys are also extremely busy people, who usually have hundreds of cases for which they are responsible. They are also responsible for what you, as a legal assistant, do. This can get so overwhelming that the office atmosphere becomes claustrophobic to some attorneys, as they not only have to worry about their workload and performance, but about yours as well.

So, then, it's everyone into high gear—and high stress!

I, being the idealist, am of the opinion that there are rare "true emergencies" in the practice of law. We all know, way ahead of time, witness list deadlines, trials, discovery cut-offs and the like. Extraordinary is the deadline that just "pops up."

Despite knowing what you and your attorney should be doing next month and maybe you as a legal assistant putting your best effort forward to complete the tasks, truthfully, staying ahead and working at a nice, even pace hardly ever happens, unless you happen to practice in one of the slower paced areas of law we discussed earlier. You can prepare that witness list three weeks in advance, but you can bet even money that it will sit on the attorney's desk until 4:47 p.m., on the Friday afternoon of that third week.

Why do I paint this picture, sometimes bleak, in shades of gray?

Because I know *you* will plan your work, but there is only so much of your career and job duties you can control. There are other people's habits, no matter how bad, you must deal with, as well as emergencies, or perceived emergencies, and staying flexible is a part of getting along with those people and absorbing the often hectic tempo.

As a legal assistant, no matter how organized, efficient and proficient you strive to be, you must also be accommodating and adaptable, learn to deal with emergencies, whether true or not, high, sudden stress, and, "Do it now!" demands.

I have found that attorneys really look to their legal assistants, more than the general public would know, to "think" for them. They look to their loyal staff to organize their practices and their lives, basically. If you can do so, with a "good sport" attitude most of the time, you will be incalculably sought after and admired.

It does get frustrating from time to time, and I have been in tears and had chest tightness more than once due to tremendous pressure to get things done, but at those times, I eventually learned to talk myself into gaining some perspective. Have I ever not been able to get something done? What if I don't get this done? What's the worst thing that could happen? Then I tell myself I can do it, and then, I just do it, not to sound like an ad for a reputable shoe company. And you know what? I have *always* been able to handle anything and get everything done. Maybe not right away, but ultimately, it all gets done. Perspective and confidence in yourself is key.

In any event, planning ahead and prioritizing work, and using these skills to keep your attorney informed and the work flowing, is essential to a good working relationship and a good working environment and should reduce the "crises" to a bare minimum.

# 4. BE ARTICULATE/DEVELOP GOOD WRITING SKILLS

This is what I call a, "Do-it-every-time" skill. Before turning over any work to your attorney, proofread and spell check everything! Every page. Every inch of text. An "and" in place of an "or" could spell disaster. Check for grammar, punctuation, general tone and style. Have a colleague look at it, if you are able, perhaps exchange documents, because sometimes others will see a mistake, where you have missed it thirty times.

Your involvement in drafting of various legal documents will also be relatively technical and practical, but here also, you can interject some creativity and spark to make your arguments and comments come alive. Try to glean and hearten some real life anecdotes and personal experiences into your demand letters and the like. Use colorful language, and where applicable or warranted, even inflammatory and graphic descriptive terminology. This tactic may spark curiosity and burn on the brain of someone you are trying to convince.

Good speaking skills will play a vital role in your career. Speak concisely. Try to eliminate "ahs" and "ums" from your speech. Remember your public speaking classes? If not, or if you have never taken such a course, take one, or read a book as a refresher. Be prepared, informed and know your material.

Even if you are just in the hallway and the senior partner is coming toward you, don't slur sloppily such as, "S' nice mornin' huh?" Say clearly and bright-eyed, "Good morning sir," or, "Good morning Amanda," or whatever your firm culture dictates. And always speak concisely and calmly on the phone with clients, other lawyers, and others. Slipping a grin on your face really does do the trick when answering the phone on a hectic day.

If you feel like you need a boost in the writing and/or speaking departments, sign up for a public speaking, business or legal writing course, head to a library, or check out the innumerable resources on the web for available information on writing and speaking styles. Sometimes sounding eloquent and making your writings clear and unambiguous is already half the battle.

# 5. BECOME "THICK-SKINNED"

This trait has to be the absolute most difficult one to master, and one that only you as an individual can master. As I stated previously in this book, I failed miserably at it for years. And I still do, albeit to a much lesser extent, thankfully. I used to internalize every little thing and beat the proverbial dead horse long after it was cold and in the ground.

I am a self-professed perfectionist, Type A, uptight sort. And I am my own worst enemy and toughest critic. If someone didn't talk to me—I jumped to the conclusion that it meant they hated me. If my boss pointed out a mistake—that must mean that I was about to be fired. If I made a mistake and I caught it—I was stupid and didn't deserve a job.

Ugh! All this exactness is exhausting! I have recently, through many years of self-torment and now, self realization, learned the lesson that not everyone or everything can or has to be perfect! And I learned a long time later that I don't even want to be perfect— because being perfect means you will never learn further. Mistakes breed wisdom.

But letting things roll off you is easy when it comes naturally, and nearly impossible when it doesn't. If you are like me, and it is like pulling teeth to loosen up, I learned that to deal with it you must change yourself. I changed how I dealt with these events. I used the professional athletes mantra to, "Park it!" I parked it in my mind, in a garden, under a box, up in a tree, anywhere that I could mentally let it go and move on. It worked for me, albeit with some practice.

Sometimes, I just let myself be upset for a while. If I was upset, I would simply tell my boss to allow me an hour or so to be upset and then I will get over it. If I tried to fight my feelings, for me, it would just be worse. So, I permitted myself to wallow in self-pity, but only for a little while! Then, I moved on and time allowed me to put things into perspective.

# 6. DOCUMENT EVERYTHING

If you have a photographic memory—great.

For the rest of us, you no longer have to rely on your memory when trying to recall every nitpicking detail about upwards of two hundred cases.

Use what is arguably the greatest invention of mankind ever, and your greatest ally—writing.

The very first phone call, project or assignment you receive, write the details down. Pen as many particulars as you can. Do this every single time. It may take some getting used to writing down and summarizing every single phone conversation, meeting, or instruction, but doing so will relieve your brain from stressing about remembering an overwhelming load of information. No single person can remember everything. And you won't have to if you write things down. Just be sure to remember where you put your papers and notes!

When writing memos or notes to myself, I like to include the name of the client or project, the date assigned, the date it is due, and any special notations. Scribble any thoughts that pop into your head, when you are "in the moment" for future reference. Thoughts that just spontaneously pop into your head when you are thinking or doing something in particular are usually right on.

Every time I got off the phone with a client, opposing counsel, adjuster, or anyone else involved in the case, I typed my note summarizing my conversation. It needn't be fancy or anything resembling fine literature. Just the facts.

For example, if I spoke with a client about their deposition, I would type something such as, "@ 2:45 p.m., TC (Telephone conference) with client re: confirming depo tomorrow." If a problem arose, say with the client not showing up, I (or anybody else in the firm with access to the file) simply had to pull up my notes and let my boss know that I had indeed spoken and confirmed with our client. Again, you should always document for other people—those who may be working on the case and those who may cover for you if you are out sick or on vacation.

This skill has helped me, and the attorneys and staff I have worked with, in immeasurable ways. Especially when starting a new job, or in a new department, it is crucial to be up to speed and reading notes is a great way to do just that.

Follow up and confirming letters are formal ways of documentation, and will also be your best weapon against memory lapses and the passing of time. For major events, such as extensions on discovery, stipulations, agreements, or any offer or demand for money, it is always best to formalize it in a letter or other type of written documentation.

## 7. DEVELOP PEOPLE SKILLS

As a "newbie" to the field of legal assisting, finding a mentor can be invaluable both to your career and personally. Find a senior paralegal at your firm, or a paralegal at a local association, or even another employee at your firm, such as a lawyer, or office manager. Once that tough, ASAP assignment lands in your lap and you are truly clueless, you can turn to this trusted person to either help you directly, or at least lead you down the right path.

If you are a veteran, one of the best ways to help out others in the legal assisting profession is to become a mentor. How do you go about doing this? Seek out a new hiree and take him or her to lunch during their first week or two on the job. You can give valuable insight and may gain a trusted ally. Being a mentor is personally fulfilling and chances are, your boss will take notice and make a mental mark of your leadership skills.

Later in my career, I had the wonderful experience of being a mentor. I feel I had many mentors on my own road to success, even though some never even knew it. I had a legal assistant who always had a smile and time for me. No matter what the question. Now, I do that for others. I smile, sit back, even if I am super busy and take the time to teach. I strive to explain procedures and complicated matters slowly and methodically in a down to earth manner, Being able to give back to someone is a wonderful feeling, and you know what? It makes my own life easier! The more your coworkers and staff know, and the more people around you who can help and are competent, the better off you will be. You do have to take vacations and get sick every now and then, of course!

Flexibility, tolerance and a good attitude will also serve you well in this field with lots of different, sometimes eruptive personalities.

I am also a proponent of being well-rounded as a paralegal, not only in the legal field, but in life and common sense as well. Actually, just being a legal assistant and working in the legal field and meeting the various personalities will likely make you considerably more versed in how the world works as your career progresses. But these skills, some call well-read, worldly, or even intuitive, insightful or instinctive, will help you sense if a client is telling the truth, a co-worker is trying to sabotage you within your firm, or if a witness is shady. You know how something just doesn't, "Pass the smell test," even if you don't *really* yet know what is truth and what is fiction? Deciphering and learning human nature will sharpen your people skills, as will studying their behaviors and possible motivations. Tuning in to people's body language, uneasiness, and potential gains or losses will, sometimes, plug you into the real story. This expertise takes time, but once polished, will serve you extremely well in this career arena.

# 8. DILIGENCE

At 4:00 p.m. or 4:30 p.m., when you are thinking about wrapping up your day, complete just one more task. Schedule a hearing, prepare a notice of deposition and subpoena, or return phone calls. This will allow you to get more things done and your attorney will notice. Keep moving is my calling card. Sometimes this is supremely difficult especially when the internet is so easy to log on to and e-mailing friends seems the perfect distraction.

Diligence, however, is one trait that is invaluable as a paralegal, and in the high-paced world of legal services in general. I worked with a legal assistant several firms back who was somewhat new to the field. While she did not have lots of work experience, she had superb work ethics, including diligence. If I assigned her a task, I absolutely knew that she would either, a) get it done, or b) find a way to get it done, or c) if all else fails, ask me or someone else if she ran into trouble. But, I always knew she would follow up and complete a task or ask someone for help to complete it. Reliability, trustworthiness and diligence are keys to success.

From your first day as a paralegal or even at a new firm, diligence can dominate. As I have tried hard to drill into you in this book, start by writing everything down. I was always impressed by new hires writing down what I was saying about the file set-ups, phone systems, and copy machine codes. How is anyone supposed to remember all that stuff when you're already overwhelmed and nervous with starting a new job?

Of course, everyone has a learning curve of a few days to couple of months to settle into a new job, but being thorough and industrious and writing down notes from day one, is a great way to start chipping away at your own learning curve and ultimately, make your own life easier.

For those with more responsibility and experience, stepping up when needed, truly going above and beyond, is the ultimate in diligence. What do I mean? Crunch times, when the firm is cranking out work, papers are flying through the copy machine and out of the printers, and the piles of work on your desk grow— even bigger(!), happen intermittently. At these times, rolling up your sleeves and just getting to work is critical for reducing those piles and getting a grip. Stepping up means, if you're really busy, coming in early. Staying late. Or working through a lunch hour. I know, I know, none of us wants this to happen *that* often, and if it happens all the time or every day, then there is probably a serious workflow, staffing or time and organization problem. But for those occasional crunch periods, step up to the challenge and go the extra mile. You will be noticed and appreciated. And the crunch time will pass.

## 9. THE "FIND OUT" MIND SET

If you cannot unearth something, training yourself to "find out" is one of the keys to standing out. Ask pertinent questions to your attorney, or your client, and know exactly what you are looking for. If finding the answer to your puzzle eludes you, ask someone who couldn't help you if they have another recommendation as to who to call. See the section above on Resourcefulness as this "find out" mind set is similar.

Ask yourself what other sources could yield this information. There is usually more than one web site, company or expert for a particular topic. Call a friend. Call a friend of a friend. Local libraries, colleges and universities, and the good ol' phone book are supremely helpful tools. If you've hit a dead end, call a colleague or use another resource, just keep going and going until you find what you need, or as close as possible. Think outside of the box to obtain the information you need.

## 10. KEEP UP WITH CHANGES

Changes occur all the time in the workplace, and can be delightful, harmful, or varying degrees in between. But they happen, and a good number of these transformations are going to be out of your control. Keeping a good and healthy attitude about change is important. If your firm implements a new voice mail system, learn the updated options rather than complaining about how you liked the old system better. Investigate and teach yourself e-mail technology and to use the vast resources of the internet. Technology is designed to enhance, not hurt. As my sister, a stand-out legal assistant, says, "I sometimes don't like what is being changed, but you must be open to change, as it is inevitable, especially when dealing with attorneys. If you get a new computer program—just learn it."

Keeping up with changes also means keeping up with technology. You may be no longer computer-wary, but do you know the latest in voice mail technology or video-conferencing for use in depositions? If you would like to learn more, become more efficient at a particular software program or are still calling a computer "the machine," consider taking a technical or software course.

Another good rule of thumb is to always keep your resume fresh, up to date and ready to send out. Keep revising it as you move jobs, earn degrees, awards or accolades, or learn another computer program. A ready-to-go resume will be your tried and true defense turned offense—you never know what can happen—perhaps layoffs or a spectacular opportunity at the best firm in town recently opened up and you want to get a jump on the competition. I always peruse the Sunday classified paper for jobs, not because I am actively seeking other employment, but because I always gathered some glimmers from firms who needed workers, firms who were expanding, or new firms cropping up. I also liked to keep up with the listed salaries in my area for the certain areas of law, and the general demand for employees.

One of the best ways of keeping up with the ever-occurring changes in procedures and case law in the legal field can be by attending seminars, sometimes called Continuing Legal Education, which all attorneys must take in order to maintain their licenses to practice law. To some people, seminars are ways to sign in, read a magazine, or blaze *outta there* to catch a movie, lunch with a friend, or to catch up on your ironing. But seriously, seminars are invaluable ways to pick up nuances about the profession, recent changes in caselaw or statutory law, hone your skills and become more of an expert in a particular area of law.

Here are some tips for getting the most out of a seminar: first, sign in and stay. Obvious? Well, as said above, your cohorts may try to get you to go shopping at the big sale going on *right now*, but you should stay to actually learn something. The speakers put a lot of effort into coming up with mostly lively, informative topics and ways to present them. Seminars are also good networking opportunities and give you a chance to get to know other members of the legal community—even judges, mayors and local business people sometimes speak at such events.

Second, listen well to the updates on case law or procedures, and keep an ear out for stories of real-life examples being told by the speakers. These often are gems of knowledge and insight. And read the materials and handouts and save them for future reference.

Third, take your business cards, if you have any, to hand out and follow up on any contacts you have made. If you liked a particular speaker, plan to e-mail him or her afterwards to let them know. Everyone likes to be complemented.

Finally, sometimes vendors such as legal software, court reporters, etc., sponsor seminars. Take the time to browse their displays or brochures and take them back to the office for the administrative files. You never know what you are going to need tomorrow or in two years. Likewise, if your firm is seeking, say, case management software, here's your chance to get some free demo time and ask questions one on one with a representative.

All in all, with a seminar or class, like the old rule of life, you get out of it what you put into it.

Yes, change is constant, sometimes welcome; sometimes cruel. But it is guaranteed at some point and if you go with the flow, be prepared and make contingency plans, your internal river of turmoil will not drop over the falls. And if the change coming your way is wonderful, you will have, by being prepared and confident, stood out from the rest of the pack to embrace it.

# VI

# CONCLUSION

The field of legal assisting has been a great choice for me and countless others. Hopefully, at this point, I have given you a fair, realistic view, haven't completely scared you off and you are excited about diving right in and starting your legal assisting career!

This profession has allowed me to touch the lives of many and has brought rewards both financially and personally. I have learned immense amounts of information about our world, people, dynamics of life in modern society and our legal system. I am proud to be a part of it and to pass on my knowledge and experiences.

I will always remember working on the poignant cases: the drawn-out and spiteful divorce, the critically wounded child victim of a car accident, the signing of a Last Will and Testament by a man soon to undergo brain surgery with only a 30% chance of living through the ordeal. This career will allow you to help someone or a family through these and countless other challenges and try to make something good come of them.

The best part about the cases you will work on, I believe, is when they are concluded. Conclusion brings closure to people's lives and somehow, even if it is not exactly what they expected, their lives are happier and less stressful with the finality of a case.

You, as a paralegal, will likely be the person these people most often speak with and deal with. If you implement your caring and bring to them your confidence and skills, they are almost always supremely appreciative.

Legal assisting can also be used as a road to another career, like I pursued for myself. I am now following my true passion, writing, and combining it with my skills as a paralegal. The paralegal field has helped me get to where I wanted to go and to where I am today. I know it will also lead me to my future.

Other legal assistants I know have used this career choice as a springboard to law school or even into the medical or insurance fields. If you are changing careers from one profession to being a legal assistant, you may be able to combine a lot of the knowledge that you already have. A nurse can be most helpful and feel right at home in a medical malpractice firm. A corporate type may settle into a corporate law firm or as a paralegal to an in-house counsel for a company. Do you like sales? Help drum up contacts and build your firm's business-networking. I know of many people who have changed careers to legal assisting, but I do not hear of many who leave the paralegal field. Those who do, usually become attorneys themselves.

If you decide this career track is right for you, I believe that you have a very bright future ahead, with superb job growth and opportunities, and you now know first-hand what to expect and what the career is actually like, through my relating some of my personal experience. You may even be leaning towards a particular area of the law to mesh with your interests or personality. Have fun!

If you decide that it doesn't sound like your path after all, at least you have learned about it from the inside and best of luck in whatever you do.

Most all of the paralegals I have met are very professional and dedicated, and they are passionate about their work. They sail through the fun, interesting cases and situations and drift through the difficult and stressful times with grace and understanding.

Legal assisting is a great career with exploding potential, and can bring a lifetime of career satisfaction.

As legal assistants, we can make a world of difference and lend a hand keeping the legal gears of justice oiled and churning at full momentum, all from the vital and wonderful vantage point—Behind the Bar.

# LIST OF RESOURCES FOR FURTHER INFORMATION

## PROFESSIONAL ORGANIZATIONS:
- National Federation of Paralegal Associations (www.nfpa.org)
- National Association of Legal Assistants (www.nala.org)

## EDUCATION:
- http://www.allparalegalschools.com
- http://www.careerschooldirectory/com/pages/adminsec/paralegal.htm
- http://www.education-online-search.com/legal_training/paralegal_ school /paralegalschools.html
- http://www.searchforcolleges.net/Legal-and-Paralegal-Programs.htm
- http://www.career-education.info/paralegal-programs.htm
- Your local Community College

## PUBLICATIONS:
- *Legal Assistant Today* (www.legalassistanttoday.com)
- *The National Paralegal Reporter* (www.nfpa.org)
- *Facts & Findings* (www.nala.org)